JOB

**BIBLE STUDY
COMMENTARY**

BOOKS IN THE BIBLE STUDY COMMENTARY SERIES

JOB

BIBLE STUDY
COMMENTARY

D. DAVID GARLAND

ZONDERVAN
PUBLISHING HOUSE
OF THE ZONDERVAN CORPORATION
GRAND RAPIDS, MICHIGAN 49506

JOB: Bible Study Commentary

Copyright © 1971 by Zondervan Publishing House, Grand Rapids, Michigan

Seventh printing 1981
ISBN 0-310-24863-9

Library of Congress Catalog Card Number: 70-156242.

The American Standard Version of the Bible
is used in quoting from the Scriptures.

Printed in the United States of America.

To
JANE AND DAVID
in whom their parents have great hope.

CONTENTS

PREFACE

This is not a critical guide to the book of Job. It is an attempt to present the main ideas of the book. To be of maximum value this volume should be read alongside the open Bible.

I am indebted to Zondervan for requesting the manuscript, to the administration of Southwestern Baptist Theological Seminary for the privilege of a leave in Zurich, Switzerland, where it was prepared, to Mr. Ernest Johnson of South Africa, my family and others who have helped me in the work.

It is hoped that the lessons to be learned from Job may be learned by all of us who will inevitably suffer one day.

D. DAVID GARLAND

CHAPTER ONE

Introducing Job and the Book

1. Job the Man
2. Job the Name
3. Job in the Canon
4. The Date of the Book
5. The Subject of the Book
6. The Integrity of the Book

The book of Job belongs to that portion of the Old Testament known as Wisdom Literature. Job, along with Proverbs, Ecclesiastes and some of the Psalms comprise this section.

Wisdom Literature, which was the literature produced by the wise men is divided into two categories. The first, and simpler of the two, is called lower wisdom. This is because of its emphasis upon the more practical rules for living — those basic rules of life which are accepted by most men and which if followed result in success. Proverbs is the Old Testament example of this type of literature.

The second type of Wisdom Literature is known as higher wisdom. It is so designated because its reflective nature and its emphasis upon the ultimate issues of human existence are considered to belong to a higher realm of wisdom than that associated with lower wisdom. Job and Ecclesiastes are the Old Testament examples of this type of writing.

Both Job and Ecclesiastes are concerned with ultimate issues. While Job is more person oriented, Ecclesiastes is more theoretical — more philosophical — oriented more toward ideas. Since man is a reflective being and concerned with the issues that affect him, Job has greater appeal for him than Ecclesiastes. The book mirrors at least one aspect of most men's lives. That is, sooner or later, the majority of us come to a place in our experience where the simple, practical or traditional solutions to the issues which confront us may no longer suffice. Life seems to have become more complicated than to allow for such simple solutions. At times, in fact, the problems appear to be insoluble. Many are therefore searching for more profound and more meaningful explanations.

Job was one who had difficulty with the traditional reasons given for suffering. In fact, he believed that there had to be a better explanation than the one being offered by his friends. Therefore he rejected their attempts to help him. He debated with them and finally with God, hoping that he would, at last, learn the real reason for his suffering, but to no avail. Such knowledge was not forthcoming. In fact, according to the story, Job never did learn that God had permitted Satan to test him. Had he known, no doubt the story would have been quite different.

Job has not been the only man to suffer without knowing the reason. Multitudes have and do suffer without ever finding an altogether satisfactory explanation. Because of this, the book of Job contributes much to any effort to understand the problem of suffering. Any person who attempts to come to grips with heartbreaks and disappointments, and tries to understand them, will greatly profit by a study of Job. It is with this in mind that our study guide is prepared. First, a look at some introductory matters:

1. *Job the Man.* The historicity of Job has been variously contested through the centuries. As early as the third century there were those who doubted that he had actually lived. He was believed to be no more than a parabolic figure.

Later, the same general position was taken by some who
held that Job and the accounts of his experiences were but
a collection of parables depicting the sufferings of the nation
of Israel. Both of these theories have been challenged, however, and there are many who favor regarding Job as an
individual who really lived, in a certain time and place in
history.

The accounts of Job's inner struggle and the situation in
which he lived are given as evidences to support his historicity. But that is not all. There are evidences outside the
book of Job which favor his personal identity. For example,
Ezekiel mentions Job in association with Daniel and Noah
(Ezekiel 14:20) as a worthy example of piety. Whether one
accepts Daniel as the Daniel of the book or the Daniel of
Ugarit, as some do, he is forced to accept the possibility of
historicity. If, then, the references to Daniel and Noah are
historical, why is not the same true of Job?

There is yet another biblical evidence used to support the
claim that Job was historical. It is found in James 5:11. Here
is a reference based upon the obvious belief of the author
of James that such a person as Job had lived and could be
used as a model of patience (see Job 1:21; 2:10). Whatever
one's position on the New Testament usage of the Old Testament, it would seem to be clear enough that the James
reference was intended to be a personal and historic one.
Otherwise, there would have been little reason for the
reference.

There are those holding to the historicity of Job who place
him in the patriarchal period. They do so for two reasons.
The first is the absence of any references to the religious
and cultural institutions of Israel. These, it is insisted, were
founded by Moses centuries after the patriarchs. Since they
are not referred to in the book of Job, it is reasoned that Job
lived before Moses, their founder.

A second reason suggested for placing Job in the patriarchal period is the obvious parallel between the life and
manner of the patriarchs in Genesis 12:50 and that depicted
in the book of Job. Because of these similarities, Job is cast

in the role of a patriarch whose wealth and family are unquestionably like those of Abraham, Isaac and Jacob.

2. *Job the Name.* The earliest known appearance of the name, Job, is in a list of Mari kings dating from 2000 to 1800 B.C. On the basis of the occurrence of 'ybm in this list and after careful study, it has been determined that 'ybm is the equivalent of the biblical name Job ('Iyyob). Centuries later, in materials from the Amarna Age (1400 B.C.) the name was also found. Here "Ayab" occurs as the name of a prince and again it was determined to be the equivalent of Job ('Iyyob).

Even though these equivalents exist, no claim is made that either individual was the Job of the Bible. The lists simply reveal that the name was in use at least as early as the time of the patriarchs.

The meaning and derivation of Job's name is not as easily discovered as that of other Old Testament persons. There seem to be two basic possibilities for the meaning of Job. The first derivative is from a Hebrew term which expresses the idea of "enmity," "the hated one" or "the persecuted one." The other possibility is from an Arabic root which means "the penitent one." Either of these possibilities would be appropriate and if there is a linguistic kinship between the two, both meanings may be applicable.

3. *The Place of Job in the Canon.* The inclusion of Job in the Hebrew canon has gone virtually unchallenged. In the fourth century, Theodore of Mopsuestia, bishop of Antioch, denied that Job was inspired but he was quickly challenged and his denial refuted. Since then, no serious objection has been made to the inclusion of Job in the canon.

Though the inclusion of Job in the canon has been almost universally accepted, the position of the book in relation to Psalms and Proverbs has not remained fixed. In the Talmud and Codex Alexandrinus the order of the books is Psalms, Job and Proverbs. The Vulgate gives the order as Job, Psalms and Proverbs. The Masoretes placed Psalms first, then Proverbs and, finally, Job. Since the Council of Trent (1545-

1563) the order has remained Job, Psalms and Proverbs in the western church.

4. *The Date of the Book.* Job's family, his possessions and his apparent personal role as patriarch revealed in the prose portions of the book prompted the belief that Moses was the author of Job. This was, of course, based upon a prior belief that Moses was responsible for the stories of the patriarchs.

If a date from the time of Moses is the earliest to be suggested for Job, then one from c. 100 B.C. would surely be the latest. This latter date is based upon the unlikely assumption that Job 15:20ff. is a reference to Alexander Jannaeus, king of Judah from 103-76 B.C. But Job had been referred to in Ecclesiasticus as early as 180 B.C. and any presumed evidence for a later date would be offset by that.

Since Wisdom Literature flourished during the reign of Solomon, some would date Job during that era. The Solomonic period was a rather peaceful and leisurely one and may have provided the most favorable period for the formulation of reflective literature. If this is granted, then it is reasoned that Job, the greatest of such works, must have been produced during that time.

Though there are reasons (which seem to be defensible) for holding to a Solomonic date for Job, there are those who object on the grounds that the theology of the book is too advanced to permit such a date. Such scholars claim that the emphasis upon individualism, the suffering of the righteous, the high ethical standards and the lofty monotheism of Job appear later than Solomon. They are, in fact, assigned to the period between the seventh and fifth centuries B.C. So Job must be dated somewhere in this general period, according to these scholars.

Even though many agree that the theological arguments of Job are a formidable basis for dating, it should be noted that the evidences for a Solomonic date are not as inconsequential as some seem to suggest. Even so, agreement on the date of Job is still a point at which unanimity is lacking.

5. *The Subject of the Book.* The subject of the book of
Job is generally held to be the problem of suffering. Some,
attempting to be more specific, suggest that the central idea
is the suffering of the righteous and, to be sure, at first reading, this would appear to be the case. But there are other
emphases in the book as well. There is the idea that man
serves God because it pays to do so or that suffering has disciplinary value. Also, some suggest that there seems to be a
de-emphasizing of the idea that when man suffers it is because of sin. In light of these several possibilities it may not
be proper to speak of a single emphasis in Job. Yet, if one is to
be sought, it must be inclusive enough to incorporate each of
the themes mentioned above. In that case, the most likely
possibility would be that of the questionable and unsatisfac-
tory theology of Job's friends or, to put it another way, the
tragedy of a restricted theology.

6. *The Integrity of the Book.* The matter of the integrity
or unity of Job has been treated in various ways. A number
of Old Testament scholars believe that the prologue and
epilogue of the book consist of an ancient legend which has
been used as the framework for the entire book. This is based
upon the supposition that the speeches in the book are concerned with Job's inner struggle while the prologue and epilogue are concerned with his material circumstances. As a
result of these differences it is held that the two divisions
were not by the same author. This theory is believed to be
supported by the fact that the prologue and epilogue are
written in prose while the remainder is in poetry; and the
use of Yahweh as the divine name in the prose section while
El, Eloah and Elohim are used as the names for God in the
poetic section, is also cited. It is also held that the prologue
and epilogue deal with Job's trial and triumph while the remainder of the book is concerned with the justice of the divine government. Since both emphases would not have come
from the same pen, it is argued, then more than one must
have been involved in the writing of Job.

The arguments for diversity of authorship are not limited

just to those sections discussed above, however. Some scholars hold that the Elihu speeches were not a part of the original poetic section of the book. This is based upon the assumptions that the speeches occur without any advance warning, that they disrupt the transition of the poem from the cycle of speeches to the Yahweh speeches, that the language is not the same as that in the other sections, and that Elihu's address contradicts the purpose of the poet which was to show that there was no ultimate solution to the problem of suffering.

In spite of what may appear to be weighty evidence to the contrary, there are sound reasons for defending the speeches. First, it is questionable whether transitions are required for the appearance of a new character in the story. After all, there was no advance warning when Satan appeared. Too, it could not be expected that Elihu would use the same language as the three friends. Also, it is questionable whether the purpose of the poet was to present an impression that there was no solution to the problem of suffering. This may not have been the case at all. The emphasis may have been to show that at times, suffering, rather than having a human reason, has a divine reason. In that case, it would be at least partially correct to say that Yahweh brought Job's suffering upon him to prove Satan wrong or even to impress Job with the idea that suffering did not need a human reason. Whether these are the facts in the case or not, they have as much basis of proof, if not more, than the so-called evidences to the contrary.

Besides the sections already referred to, the poem on wisdom in chapter 28 has been denied as the work of the original author. This denial is based on the belief that had Job been knowledgeable enough to speak with such profundity, it would have been unnecessary for Yahweh to point him to wisdom as He did in chapters 38-41. Yet, just the opposite would seem to be the case. The wisdom expressed in chapter 28 provides a perfect occasion for Job's knowledge to be seen in its true light. In that case, this knowledge was much less than he had presumed it to be. Nevertheless, and as impor-

tant as chapters 38-41 seem to be to the overall picture, they
have, also, been denied as the work of the original author.
In this case the denial is based upon the alleged "unevenness"
found in the addresses. Presumably this can be seen in several so-called disruptions. First, it is contended that the de-
scriptions of the crocodile and hippopotamus fit poorly into
the context. The fact that Yahweh speaks twice from the
storm is held to disrupt the pattern of the book. Finally, the
precipitous submission of Job to Yahweh is believed to con-
tribute to the "unevenness" of the book. But are these pre-
suppositions valid? Those who contend for the unity of the
book, and there is ample reason to do so, believe that the
so-called unevenness, the unnecessary repetitions and the
precipitous appearances, rather than calling for diversity of
authorship form a continuous narrative which has come from
the hand of the author at various stages in his life.

FOR FURTHER STUDY

1. Read the article on "Job, Book of" in the *Interpreter's
Dictionary of the Bible* (from this point on referred to as
IDB), Volume II, pp. 911-924 and the article on "Job" in the
second edition of the Hasting's *Dictionary of the Bible* (from
now on referred to as *DB*), pp. 501-505. Also see the article
on "Job" in *The Zondervan Pictorial Bible Dictionary*, edited
by Merrill C. Tenney, pp. 433-434 (referred to as *ZPBD*).

2. Read the articles on "Wisdom" in *IDB*, Volume IV,
pp. 852-860 and in *DB*, pp. 1039-1040.

3. Read the article on "Ugarit" in *IDB*, Volume IV, pp.
724-732 and the one on "Ras Shamra Tablets" in *DB*, pp.
833-834.

4. Read the articles on "Mari" in *IDB*, Volume III, pp.
264-266 and in *DB*, p. 618.

5. Read the articles on "Tell El-Amarna" in *IDB*, Volume
IV, pp. 529-533, and in *DB*, p. 960.

6. Read the articles on "Talmud" in *IDB*, Volume IV, pp.
511-515 and in *DB*, pp. 954-956.

CHAPTER TWO
The Prologue
(Job 1:2-2:13)

1. An Introduction to Job and His Family (1:1-5)
2. The First Heavenly Council Meeting (1:6-12)
3. Job's Loss of His Possessions and Children (1:13-22)
4. The Second Heavenly Council Meeting (2:1-6)
5. Job's Personal Affliction (2:7-10)
6. The Arrival of Job's Friends (2:11-13)

The book of Job opens with a narrative prologue. Here we are introduced to Job, to his family, to the circumstances resulting in his unbearable afflictions as well as his reactions to them and to his friends who had come to bring him comfort in his suffering. This section begins with an introduction to Job and his family.

1. *An Introduction to Job and His Family* (1:1-5). The first reference in the book is to Job, the central figure in the story. According to the record, he was from "the land of Uz." Since the reference is to "the land of Uz," and not the city of Uz, it relates to a region rather than a town or village. The size and location of the area are unknown. Other references to a place called Uz are found in the book of Lamentations where "the daughter of Edom" is said to dwell "in the land

of Uz" (Lamentations 4:21) and in Jeremiah where Uz is associated with the land of the Philistines (Jeremiah 25:20). Both of these suggest a region in the south. On the other hand, the name Uz appears in some of the genealogical lists of the patriarchs and, according to Genesis 10:23, is identified as a member of the tribe of Aram who was associated with the east rather than the south and whose lineage is probably to be traced through Nahor, the brother of Abraham (Genesis 22:20:21). In light of these references, assuming the area or town to have been named for Uz and the reference to Job's being "the greatest of all the children of the east" (1:3), it is reasonable to contend for a location somewhere in the east. In either case, the emphasis is not to be put upon the location but upon Job.

Job is referred to as one who "was perfect and upright, and one who feared God and turned from evil" (1:1). In the Hebrew the verbs for "fear" and "turn" are both participles. They suggest that Job "kept on fearing" and "kept on turning." These were the normal and consistent practices of his life. He held God in such awe and respect ("fear") that he had gained wisdom and sufficient motivation to keep him from evil as well as the resultant calamities which befall those who engage in wrong-doing. Job was a living example of the Proverb: "A wise man feareth (God), and departeth from evil . . ." (Proverbs 14:16). These characteristics were the abiding factors of his life.

To this remarkable man were born seven sons and three daughters (1:2). The construction of verse 2 makes it possible to translate the conjunction "and so" instead of "and." If this is done, then it serves to introduce a resultant clause which would read: "And so (as a result of the aforementioned) there were born to him seven sons and three daughters." In that case, the author was stating that Job's children and later his possessions, were his reward for fearing God and turning from evil. In a similar concept, the Psalmist wrote: "Blessed is everyone that feareth Jehovah, That walketh in his ways. . . . Thy children like olive plants, Round about thy table" (Psalm 128:1-3). This was the author's way of saying that to the righteous man there would be born children of promise and blessing as a reward for his good and exemplary living.

There follow, in verse 3, additional blessings resulting from Job's having "feared God, and turned away from evil." He had 7,000 sheep, 3,000 camels, 500 yoke of oxen, 500 female donkeys and an unspecified number ("great household") of servants who attended his flocks and cared for his household. Job was, in fact, "the greatest of all the children of the east."

After the listing of Job's possessions (1:2, 3) there follows a picture of the relations within his family. These are seen in the nearness of the children to each other and their obvious delight and joy in the company of one another (1:4). From their father, and probably from their mother, they had learned the joys of a vital family relationship.

Job had taught his children well, but he did not cease to be concerned with their personal relationship to God. After they were mature and responsible, Job, as head of the family, remained a vital factor in their religious life (1:5). Evidently week by week, or on other stated occasions, Job would offer sacrifices to expiate any wrongs thoughtlessly or inadvertently committed by his children during their times of banqueting or festivity. His actions do not suggest that his children had "sinned" (missed the mark) or "renounced" God (treated Him lightly) during their times of festivity. They only reveal Job's great and continued concern for their right standing before God. One might wish that the account of this idyllic picture could continue, but the scene abruptly shifts from earth to heaven and there follows a long series of events the cause of which Job is never permitted to learn.

2. *The First Heavenly Council Meeting* (1:6-12). With the shift from earth to heaven, the very direction of the book of Job changes. It was in heaven, after all, that Job's destiny was to be finally decided. On occasions, presumably set by God, the celestial beings ("sons of God") were summoned to appear before Him to give a report on their activities (1:6). The reference here, as well as another in 38:7, is clearly to

those heavenly beings who have been designated "angels" in the Septuagint. They were the personal agents or servants of God who performed such tasks as He might choose to assign them for the accomplishing of His will and purpose in heaven and on earth.

Among those assembled was Satan, "the adversary," who had traversed the earth, apparently seeking any whom he might falsely accuse or otherwise harm (1:7b). Whether Satan was there by deception, stealth or as a providential aspect of God's purpose, the story does not say. It only relates the events which transpired but at the same time the author is careful to make it clear that Satan was required to have God's permission to carry through with any of his plans.

With God's inquiry and Satan's response, the narrative turns back to Job. God asked Satan, "Hast thou considered my servant Job?" Then, He quickly and confidently characterized him as "a perfect and an upright man, one that feareth God, and turneth away from evil" before Satan could respond to His question (1:8). When Satan responded he did so with a question. He asked, "Doth Job fear God for nought?" By raising this question Satan was impugning Job's motives and suggesting that he served God because it was profitable for him to do so. After all, had not God provided him security ("built a hedge about him") in the possessions which He had given him (1:10)? All God would need to do to prove him right, so Satan believed, would be to remove all He had given Job. If this were to be done, said Satan, "he will renounce thee to thy face." In other words, Satan was contending, "There is no such thing as selfless devotion to God. Everything a man does in obedience to Him is for personal gain. If God were to cease blessing him, he would deny Him" (1:11).

As a result of Satan's false insinuations concerning Job and his implicit challenge of the righteousness in God's system of rewards, he was granted permission to put Job to the test. This readily revealed God's great confidence in Job. He did not hesitate a moment nor did He express the least doubt in the ultimate outcome of the challenge. The only restriction placed upon Satan was that he not touch Job's person. Satisfied and no doubt, gleeful, "Satan went forth from the presence of Yahweh" to prove his claim about Job (1:12). This he planned to do by destroying all of Job's possessions and taking the lives of his children.

3. *Job's Loss of His Possessions and Children* (1:13-22). Job had invested a lifetime in accumulating the cattle and other possessions in which he had found such personal satisfaction. His great wealth meant that God had looked upon him with favor. Yet, without any apparent reason so far as Job could see, all these were taken from him in swift succession. That the catastrophes were unexpected may be seen in the fact that Job's children were participating in a religious festival or in some private celebration when the disasters came. They were totally oblivious to any danger. Had they anticipated any enemy action they would have responded quite differently and would, no doubt, have died in the fields where they had gone to meet the enemy.

The first ominous report to Job was that the Sabaeans, inhabitants of a region in southwest Arabia, had fallen upon his servants who were plowing in the fields and had fled with the livestock after having slain all of the "young men," save one (1:15). While the lone survivor was reporting news of Job's loss, a second arrived with word that "fire . . . from heaven" (lightning) had consumed the sheep and all of the shepherds save himself (1:16). Before he had finished with his report, a third servant arrived to tell Job that three bands of Chaldeans (Aramean nomadic plunderers) had raided the camel flock and slain all the attendants except himself (1:17). During the report of the lone survivor of the camel raid, yet another breathless servant arrived with the gravest news of all. He brought word that Job's children had lost their lives in a whirlwind which had destroyed the "eldest brother's house" where they were participating in a religious festival or some other kind of celebration (1:18, 19).

Job was no doubt shaken by the news of each of the surviving servants, but the report of the news of the disaster which took the lives of his children left him stunned. He had been peculiarly blessed in that he had seven (a sacred number suggesting special favor) sons and three (a smaller number implying added favor) daughters. The number of sons and daughters reflect the Old Testament's favored attitude toward sons. Sons occupied a favored position because the responsibility for the perpetuation of the family name and the carrying on of the family traditions fell upon the male children. Therefore, what great hope to have had seven sons! But now Job had been denied even the promise of his children. What a devastating blow!

Upon receiving news of these disasters, Job began to give expression to his grief. His first reaction was to tear his mantle (compare Genesis 37:34, Joshua 7:6, and Ezra 9:3, 5). After he had torn his mantle, he shaved his head (an added sign of grief) and prostrated himself upon the ground to show his submissiveness and helplessness (1:20). Then, while lying prostrate, he declared that he had entered the world "naked" (without possessions) and that he would leave it the same way. All that life had afforded him had come from Yahweh and now, evidently on the basis of His sovereignty, Yahweh had recalled all that He had given him (1:21). In response to this, Job, rather than cursing God as Satan had predicted, "blessed the name of Jehovah." By so doing, he was declaring that he had not served God because it was profitable for him, yet at the same time, he acknowledged God as the source of all he possessed and he blessed Him for having given it. Now, God had taken everything away and Job could still bless Him. What a rebuke to Satan's claim! Yahweh's confidence in Job had been vindicated. "In all this Job sinned not, nor charged God foolishly" (1:22). Here the author was saying that Job had not charged Yahweh with any unworthy acts. By responding in that way he had won the first round. Satan had been demonstrated wrong but he would not give up after one try. He plotted another.

4. *The Second Heavenly Council Meeting* (2:1-6). The scene of the second council meeting is precisely as the first.

The "sons of God" had come to report on their activities since they last met (2:1). God inquires of Satan's activity and taunts him by repeating His generous evaluation of Job as well as showing His delight in Job's vindication of the confidence He had already placed in him (2:3a). Job had held fast to his integrity (2:3b). There was not the slightest indication that he could have faltered. Then God placed the responsibility for Job's predicament squarely on Satan. He accused Satan of inciting Him to give Job over to him "without cause." According to this it was all prompted by Satan's sinister motives which may have been, at least in part, provoked by Yahweh's confidence and trust in Job.

Satan, however, ignored the implications of Yahweh's charge. He turned the conversation away from himself to Job. This time he recited a proverb: "Skin for skin, yea, all that a man hath will he give for his life" (2:4). That is to say, a man has not been truly tested until his own life has been jeopardized. Satan reasons that until a man is personally and physically involved it is a secondary trial. Therefore, he suggests that if Yahweh would like to see the real character of Job He should touch him physically (2:5); then Yahweh would see him for what he really was because Job would renounce Him to His face.

Yahweh, after listening to Satan, accepted his challenge and placed Job in his hands with only one limitation. Satan must spare his life (2:6).

5. *Job's Personal Affliction* (2:7-10). Upon gaining Yahweh's permission, Satan immediately set out to break Job's will. This time he turned upon him with added vengeance. He smote him from head to foot with boils or some other type of running ulcer (2:7). The nature of the disease was such as to require Job to leave the city and live with the outcasts (2:8). Since "ashes" are mentioned, it is probably a reference to the place outside the city where ashes and refuse were dumped. If so, Job took his place among other broken men who suffered and mourned in the loneliness and anguish of rejection.

Though the exact nature of Job's illness is unknown, it was evidently accompanied by a terrible itching which he sought to relieve by scraping away the accumulated matter with a potsherd (a piece of broken pottery) (2:8a).

As Job sat upon the ash heap, we are introduced to his wife who, according to the Targums, was named Dinah. Her role in the tragedy has been disputed through the centuries. Some scholars have contended that she was the devil's advocate who served as intermediary between Satan and Job. Others have suggested that her purpose was to show how those around Job gave way under the burden of his affliction. This would further enhance the picture of his own strength. Still others have held that it was no discredit to Job's wife that her faith did not measure up to his. In fact, her faith would not have been expected to do so. After all, she had suffered the loss of children and possessions as had her husband. But to see him in such a pathetic state was more than she could be expected to endure in silence. Therefore, she called upon Job to "renounce God, and die." Whatever her motivation for doing what she did or the author's for including the account of it, Job reacted as one would expect. He charged her with speaking foolishly (1:10). He interpreted her suggestion as not necessarily meaning that she was a foolish woman but that she, under the stress of the moment, had spoken in the way a foolish woman (one lacking in moral and spiritual strength) speaks.

After his wife's suggestion and its rejection, Job sought to help her see the implications of her admonition. He did this by asking her the question: "What? Shall we receive good at the hand of God, and shall we not receive evil?" (2:10). By this question, he was suggesting that man should be just as willing to accept whatever pain God might send his way as he would be to accept the good that He sends. Evidently this was the proper attitude for Job because the author records: "In all this did not Job sin with his lips." Job had then passed the second test; Satan had again been bested.

Yet Job's trial was not over. In some ways, his greatest
test lay before him. It would come with the visit of his
friends. As well intentioned as they surely must have been,
their approach to Job's problem but added to his distress.
First, an introduction to those who had come to comfort
Job and what they found when they arrived is in order.

6. *The Arrival of Job's Friends* (2:11-13). Upon learning
of the disastrous events in the life of Job, three of his friends
made their way to his city with every intention of doing
what they could to help him (2:11). Eliphaz came from
Teman of Edom, Bildad from Shuah, probably located in
the Euphrates region, and Zophar from Naamah. Though
there is a reference to a Naamah in Joshua, it is doubted
that this was his home (Joshua 15:41). If not, then the
location is unknown.

We are not told how Job's friends received the news about
his plight nor how they communicated with each other in
planning their journey. But in due time and without cere-
mony they arrived. Upon their arrival they saw a man in
such a pathetic state they did not recognize him as their
friend. After learning this was the one they had come to
console, they rent their garments and threw dust toward
heaven as signs of mourning and inexpressible grief (2:12).
(By throwing dust heavenward it is supposed they were
acknowledging or declaring their belief that heaven was the
source of Job's distress.)

The three comforters sat in silence for seven days and
seven nights (2:13), the usual length of time set aside as a
period of mourning for one who had died (Genesis 50:10;
I Samuel 31:13). Whether this tradition was the basis of their
silence is unknown. If it was, then they were mourning for
him as though he were dead. It could have been that their
reluctance to communicate was based upon a principle
enunciated in the Talmud. There it is stated that a com-
forter is not to speak to one in mourning until after he has
spoken. On the other hand, the pathetic picture of Job
could have been the reason for their prolonged silence — or

it may have been a combination of the three. Whatever the case, one needs no further proof "that his grief was very great."

For Further Study

1. Read the article on "Uz" in *IDB*, Volume IV, p. 741, or in *DB*, p. 1021, or *ZPBD*, p. 878.

2. For a discussion of Satan, read pp. 200-306 in *The Theology of the Old Testament* by A. B. Davidson or a similar discussion in some other Old Testament Theology. *The Theology of the Older Testament* by J. Barton Payne (Zondervan) is helpful.

3. Read the article on "Seven, Seventh, Seventy" in *IDB*, Volume IV, pp. 294-295.

4. Read the article on "Suffering and Evil" in *IDB*, Volume IV, pp. 450-453 or the book entitled *The Problem of Suffering in the Old Testament* by A. S. Peake.

5. Read the articles in *IDB* on "Eliphaz," Volume II, p. 91; "Bildad," Volume I, p. 437-438; and "Zophar," Volume IV, p. 963.

CHAPTER THREE

The First Cycle of Speeches

(Job 3:1 — 14:22)

Whether the silence of Job's friends was based upon the practice that they were to await a word from the one they were mourning before speaking themselves we are not told. Neither are we told if their silence of a week reflected an attitude that Job's distress was comparable to death. In either eventuality, Job was the first to speak.

1. *Job Breaks the Silence* (3:1-26). After the period of silence in the company of his friends of former days, "Job opened his mouth, and cursed his day" (3:1). By doing so, he decried the day he was born. First, he asked that the place of the day on the calendar be abolished and, secondly, that the same fate befall the night of his conception (3:3). If the day could not be struck from the calendar, then it should be-

come a day of darkness and never be allowed to appear again as a day upon which the light would shine (3:4). He wished it to be engulfed by the terrors which at times grip the day— probably references to natural causes such as heavy clouds, or even eclipses, which change the light of day into deep darkness (3:5).

"As for the night," that is, the night of his conception, he called upon God to bring a "thick" darkness upon it and to deny it a place in reckoning the days and months of the year (3:6). He wanted it to be an empty (solitary) night, without conception, lest it be another occasion for rejoicing as when he was conceived (3:7). Job would have had the necromancers curse the day of his birth by calling upon leviathan, the monster who devours the heavenly bodies, so it could not be a day of light (3:8). Then, turning his attention once more to the night, he asked that it be denied the "stars of the twilight" and "the eyelids of the morning," that is, the long rays of morning light, because it was the beginning of the process which had brought him to his present state (3:9, 10).

After Job's condemnation of the day of his birth and the night of his conception there followed a series of questions. First, he wished to know why he had not died at the time of his birth (3:11). Had he done so, he would have found the quiet, the sleep and the rest known only to those stilled by death (3:12-16). There, the wicked are silent and the weary lie in repose (3:17). In death, the prisoner, who had been much abused by his taskmaster, would be free from the cruelty of harsh treatment and all men would be equal (3:18, 19). Job looked upon death as a deliverance from misery. His suffering had blinded him, for the moment at least, to any positive results from life. Therefore, he believed it would have been better had he died at birth.

After having raised a question about his survival at birth, Job turned, in the second place, to explore the possibility of dying in the immediate future. Since life was so filled with trouble, Job asked why he should continue to be given the light of life (3:20). He longed for death. He sought it with the kind of industry men employ when searching for treasures, and he would have rejoiced with the exultation of one who had uncovered a treasure, over the mere possibility of finding it (3:21, 22).

Job felt hedged in because the way out of his dilemma was hidden from his view (3:23). Weeping was his regular diet; his tears did not cease to pour forth in endless torrents (3:24). Somewhat like a hypochondriac, he had but to fear an affliction and it would overtake him (3:25). There was not a moment's peace for his tortured spirit. One trouble followed another (3:26). Thus, did Job describe his tormented existence. Yet, in all that he said, he did not fulfill Satan's prediction that he would curse God. He did, on the other hand, curse the day of his birth. This he did because he believed it would have been better had he not been born than that he should have been forsaken by Yahweh (compare Matthew 26:24).

2. *Eliphaz's Initial Speech* (4:1 — 5:27). Eliphaz was the first of Job's friends to speak. This fact may suggest that he was the oldest of the three. If not the oldest, he must have been the most respected of the group. Though he did not know the real reason for Job's suffering, he did have a general principle from which he worked. He believed that Job's dilemma could be explained only on the basis of some great sin which he had committed.

Eliphaz reluctantly began his speech by asking whether Job was able to listen to his observations or not (4:2). He reminded him of the innumerable occasions on which he (Job) had helped others understand their afflictions and had strengthened them as they stumbled beneath the burdens of their suffering and loss (4:3, 4). Yet, when Job encountered what those he had sought to help encountered, he reacted as he had counseled them not to react (4:5). Eliphaz wished to know why.

In verse 6, Eliphaz tells Job that piety ("fear of God") is the basis of assurance and that one's integrity (blamelessness) is the basis of hope (4:6). He reminds him that the righteous do not perish (4:7) but that those who make their work cultivating ("plowing") "iniquity" and sowing "mischief" reap what they have sown (4:8). The "breath of God," the "blast of his anger" will consume them just as surely as the desert winds consume the fields upon which they blow (4:9).

After the analogy of the field, Eliphaz drew a lesson from the relationship of the family of the lion. He depicted the disintegration of the family by contrasting the roar of the strong lion with its apparent silence after its teeth were broken (4:10). With all its strength gone, symbolized in the broken teeth, the adult lion perishes and the "whelps" scatter in search of food (4:11). Eliphaz, by the use of this analogy, was suggesting that as there is a relationship between the strong and violence, so there is a relationship between the wicked and judgment.

Following his initial reaction to Job's plight, Eliphaz recounted the contents of a dream in which he had beheld the vast difference between creation and the Creator. Evidently the dream was the result of the effort on Eliphaz's part to rationalize Job's situation.

In the darkest night, while most were fast asleep, Eliphaz had had a vision in which a voice whispered disquieting thoughts into his ear (4:12-14). The voice was associated with a breath or wind which blew over him (4:15). Such a wind is quite often associated with the divine presence in the Old Testament (see 2 Samuel 5:24). Though Eliphaz could not determine the form of the presence, he was aware of it and heard it speak (4:16). It raised two deeply profound questions (4:17): one, dealing with the issue of man being just before God, and the other, dealing with his being "pure before his Maker." Both were implicitly answered in the negative. Men, all men, are unjust and unclean in God's presence. None is as pure as He. Even the angels are vulnerable when compared with the Creator (4:18). This being the situation with the angels, how much more with man who has been created from the dust? He is as frail as a moth which may survive but a day ("betwixt morning and evening") and quickly perishes without anyone taking note of it (4:19, 20).

In a comparable moment, a man's tent-cord—his dwelling—
is plucked up (a figure of death) and he dies lacking the
wisdom which might have otherwise saved him (4:21).

In the preceding paragraph, Eliphaz had reminded Job
that man is frail and transitory. By doing so, he had suggested that it was the lot of all men to fall short of perfection.
Job was a man. It was to be expected that he should therefore possess the weaknesses of man. Since the angels were
frail creatures, could mere man expect to be less than blameless? The answer would naturally be a negative one. That
being so, Eliphaz was implying that Job had sinned. Therefore, that which had happened to Job was nothing other than
what could be expected and had now, in fact, occurred. Why
should Job, then, resist such a fact of life?

In chapter 5, Eliphaz continues with the principle revealed
in the vision. He commanded Job to call upon the angels to
see what would happen (5:1). If he had done so, there had
been no response—because verse 2 seems to be a description
of Eliphaz's reaction to Job's resultant vexation and indigna-
tion. Afterward, Eliphaz continued to press the issue upon
Job by describing the disastrous end of one who is found
guilty of sin (5:3-5). This was, he believed, what such guilty
persons should expect because man, created from the dust
and certainly not divine, was weak and sinful by nature.
When trouble comes, it should not take him by surprise or
precipitate a vexatious and indignant response. It should be
expected. As a matter of fact, it should be considered as natural as sparks flying upward from a fire (5:7).

As a result of his reasoning about Job's circumstance,
Eliphaz told Job what he would have done had he been in
his place. He would not have reacted as Job had. He would
have done just the opposite. Rather than raising any question
about God's justice or his own innocence, he would have cast
himself upon God's mercy (5:8). Having seen what God had
done in the past (5:9-16), Eliphaz believed this to be the
better course.

After making his point by stating the way he would have
reacted, Eliphaz set about to help Job see what he believed

to be the positive value in what had happened. He believed
that suffering, rather than being a thing for Job to despise,
should have been a source of happiness (5:17). It was God's
way of reminding man of his sin. This he does in order that
man can be brought to the point of acknowledging and confessing his sin, after which God binds up the wounds and re-
pairs the ruptured fellowship (5:18). In other words, Eliphaz
was saying, "God afflicts man for his own good." It reminds
him that he is human and that he must submit to God or endure the consequences. If he submits, God will bind up the
wounds and restore the penitent to a relationship of happiness and joy. But that is not all; He will provide deliverance
and security (5:19). The whole universe will become the ally
of those who submit to God. They will be delivered from
famine and war (5:20). Slander and desolation will not reach
them (5:21). Destruction, drought and famine will not
frighten them (5:22). The very stones of the field, such a
hindrance to tilling the soil, and the wild beasts which prey
upon the farmer will no longer impede, frighten, or take the
life of one who has turned to God (5:23). He will have nothing to fear. His home will not be disturbed nor will the
animals in his fold have reason to fear (5:24). The offspring
of this man will be great (5:25) and he will live a long and
full life (5:26).

After this rather lengthy list of the rewards for submitting
to God's chastening, Eliphaz concluded his speech by stating
that, after careful investigation, these things had been demonstrated to be true (5:27a). Since they were, he said to Job,
"Hear it, and know thou it for thy good" (5:27b).

3. *Job's Response to Eliphaz* (6:1 — 7:21). Though
Eliphaz had not charged Job with sin, he had implied as
much and had moreover charged him with impiety based
upon a lack of patience. In response to this, Job called for a
balancing of his grief and misfortune against "the sands of
the seas." If this were to be done, his tragic loss would out-
weigh them. It was because of this imbalance that his words
had been rash (6:2, 3). The catastrophe, referred to as the

"arrows of the Almighty," which had befallen him on every side had so saturated his being as to have challenged the very springs of life themselves (6:4). He had not cried out without cause. No creature does. The donkey and ox cry out when they are without food (6:5). It was only after life had become tasteless and insipid for him, as savorless food to the animals, that Job cried out in his distress (6:6). Existence itself no longer appealed to him. It was as food which was "loathsome" and tasteless—food which one would refuse to eat (6:7).

In light of life's circumstances, Job once again called for the realization of his desire to die (6:8, 9). This he wanted to happen soon while he was still innocent; because at the present time he had not disowned "the words of the Holy One" (6:10). His strength had become so dissipated that hardly enough remained to maintain life and there seemed to be no promise of better things in the future (6:11). After all, he was but a man. His strength was not like the strength of stone or brass (6:12). Since he did not have the inner resources to sustain him, every possibility of arriving at a way of recovery seemed cut off (6:13). Therefore, death, while he was still innocent, was Job's chief concern.

Following this outburst, Job voiced disappointment in the attitudes which his friends had shown toward him. He believed that one's friends should be kind toward him, even if, as Eliphaz had implied, he had forsaken "the Almighty" (6:14). Quite to the contrary, Job saw his friends as treacherous and unreliable like the streams of Palestine. During the rainy season they pour forth great floods of water but in the hot dry summer season, when the waters are desperately needed, they have all flowed away (6:15). In verse 16, the reference is extended to include the melting of the ice and snow of the Lebanon, Anti-Lebanon mountains and the water this affords (6:16, 17). As did Job's friends, these waters fail the thirsty desert travelers, so they turn back into the desert, confounded, with no other alternative but to perish (6:18-21). In his own case, Job had only asked for their understanding. He had anticipated their help when he

saw them arrive, just as the desert caravans had expected
to satisfy their thirst with the water of the streams—but to no
avail. They had reacted as though he had asked them for
their material resources or to risk their lives by trying to
free him from the hands of an oppressor (6:22, 23). Job had
not asked for some great feat on his behalf. He only wanted
their concern and sympathy. Thus far, they had failed him
at both points.

Having emptied his heart of his disappointment, Job called
on Eliphaz, and no doubt the others at the same time, to
show him wherein he had erred (6:24). He called for a forth-
right charge against him rather than concealed implications
(6:25). Job challenged their approach. All they had to reprove were the words of a man on the verge of despair
(6:26). Their actions had been as heartless as those dis-
played by creditors who cast lots for a dead man's children
to satisfy the obligations of the deceased or as those who
sought to "make merchandise" of their friends (6:27).

Following these severe charges, Job asked them to look at
him and see if he appeared to be one who would lie to their
faces (6:28). Surely, upon further investigation, they would
discover that he had not committed unrighteous acts (6:29).
After all, Job believed he would have known had he spoken
injustice or performed evil deeds (6:30). He did not need
the help of others to detect wrong in his own life. He was
sensitive enough to have detected it for himself had it been
present.

Through these words, Job not only declared his innocence,
he had gone a long way toward a refutation of Eliphaz's
argument. Later, he would remonstrate with God about the
hard lot of man's life on earth.

Job compared life with a time of military service in which
the mercenary soldier labors like a hireling in the field (7:1).
He eagerly awaits the end of the work day so he can escape
from the heat of the sun and receive his meager wages with
which to buy food (7:2). Life is filled with disappointments,
according to Job. Long night after long night he had tossed
about upon his bed unable to sleep (7:3, 4). His body was

wracked with pain. The ulcers, having become infested with worms and covered with dirt, had broken open, bled and added to his irritation (7:5).

Because of his condition it became obvious that Job's life was fast fleeting. It was speeding away with the speed of the weaver's shuttle and there was little if any time left for restoration (7:6). So, Job besought God to remember the transitoriness of life and the grim prospect of his ever again experiencing the good life which he had formerly known (7:7). Those who had seen him in the past, perhaps God included, would never see him again (7:8) because he would be going down to Sheol, the abode of the dead, never to reappear (7:9, 10). Because of this, Job remonstrated with God.

He began by declaring that he would not hold back anything. He would be open and frank with God (7:11). He complained of being watched as though he were some kind of monster which had to be kept in sight (7:12) and of being tormented by "dreams" and "visions" when he lay down to sleep (7:13, 14). For Job, in his condition, death was preferred to living (7:15). Loathing life, he asked God to leave him alone. Life is but a breath of wind (7:16). That being so, Job wished to know what there was about man that God should devote so much of His time afflicting him (7:17, 18). "God keeps him in his sight always," he complained. He accused Him of not looking elsewhere long enough for him to swallow his spittle unnoticed (7:19). If he had been such a sinner as to bring this kind of affliction upon himself, Job wanted to know how it could hurt God and, if it had not hurt Him, he would like to know why He was always striking out against him and making life so unbearable (7:20).

With little left to be said, Job concluded his response to Eliphaz by asking why God had not forgiven him and by reminding Him that in a brief while it would be too late; he would be gone (7:21). Whatever God planned to do it must be done soon, else there would be little need for any response on his part. With this warning, Job concluded his first response. He had then to face the charges brought by Bildad, the second friend to speak.

4. *Bildad's Initial Speech* (8:1-22). Bildad was the traditionalist among the friends. He ignored Job's anguished spirit. He wanted to know how long Job intended to continue speaking as he had — with words which were injurious and windy (8:2). Then he raised the question of God's perverting justice (8:3). By doing so, he was implying that Job's distresses were based upon his sin and not upon any fault in the action of God. Afterwards, he turned to the most painful of all Job's griefs, the death of his children. He stated his belief that they had been judged because of their transgression (8:4).

Pursuing his argument, Bildad reasoned that if Job, guilty as his children had been, would seek God and beseech Him to be merciful, that He would forgive him and restore his prosperity (8:5, 6). If Job, according to Bildad, were pure and upright then God would awake to his claim and give him a prosperity exceeding any he had ever known. In fact, his beginning would be small in comparison with his latter end (8:7).

Following his defense of the justice of God (8:2-7), Bildad appealed to the lessons of the past. Job is admonished to look at the accumulated experiences of the preceding generations and to learn from them (8:8). Bildad believed the past had many lessons for Job. One's life is too short to be involved in the total experience of the race (8:9). Therefore, Job ought to let himself be taught by those whose words had been formed in the crucible ("out of their heart") of life's deepest experience (8:10).

In 8:11-19 Bildad sets forth three proverbs which reflect the accumulated wisdom of the past. The first was the proverb of the "papyrus" and "reed grass" (8:11-13). It dealt with questions of whether papyrus can grow without mire or the reed without water (8:11). The answer of the proverb is that they cannot. They would wither before they had produced their fruit, that is, before the time when they

were ripe for harvesting (8:12). Just as these plants perish
without "mire" and "water" so will men perish who do not
depend upon the resources and favor of God (8:13). In
other words, man is as dependent upon God as plants are
dependent upon "mire" and "water."

Next, Bildad used the proverb of the spider web. Here,
by analogy, he pointed out that those who refuse to turn
to God are as insecure and helpless as a spider web which
has been cut from its moorings (8:14, 15).

The last proverb is of the gourd. The wicked man is compared to the gourd which grows rapidly and sends its roots
down into the stones expecting to be secure, but if the gourd
is "destroyed from his place," then the undisturbed nature
of the stones, after it has been uprooted, would deny that
a vine had ever been there (8:16-18). So it is with the
wicked man. He flourishes for a while. Afterwards, there
is no evidence of his having existed. Then follows the ironic
statement in verse 19 which states that such a man's joy will
be brief — as brief as the life of the vine which has been
uprooted and quickly replaced by another (8:19).

In verses 20-22, Bildad made a further application of
the proverbs recounted above. He re-affirmed his belief in
the justice of God by stating that He would not cast away
a righteous man nor sustain a wicked one (8:20). On the
basis of what he has already said, and by subtle implication,
Bildad suggested that Job's future would be filled with happiness and joy in a circumstance in which he would be delivered from his enemies and in which the wicked would be
eliminated (8:22). But these conditions would depend upon
Job's following his (Bildad's) advice. Having been convinced of Job's guilt, Bildad could not see him restored to
his former state without his acknowledging and confessing
his sin. His promise of the future was predicated upon
Job's confession. Thus, Job has been told once again what
he had already heard, but this time, with the added weight
of tradition.

5. *Job's Response to Bildad* (9:1 — 10:22). Job opened

his response to Bildad by making an acknowledgment and asking a question. He acknowledged the principle that God does not forsake the righteous but he wished to know how it was possible for man to be judged righteous by God (9:2). Man cannot answer one out of a thousand questions raised by Him (9:3). By this, Job suggested that should man wish to contend with God, because of his plight, he would be unable to defend himself against one out of a thousand charges which God could bring against him. This is because God is wise and strong. No one can challenge Him and prosper since God would always come out the winner and the one challenging Him would always be the loser (9:4).

After having stated his belief that man would lose in a match with God, Job turned to a description of the power of God in the realm of nature. He is the one who removes mountains before they realize what has happened (9:5a). With the earthquake, He shakes the earth to its very pillars and they respond by shaking as though gripped by terror (9:6). God controls the light of the sun and the twinkling of the stars (9:7). They rise and shine at His command. He created the heavens and walks about upon the high places ("waves") of the sea (9:8). It was God who created the constellations and the "chambers" which make up the sky of the south (9:9). In fact, Yahweh has done these things and many more, without number, and beyond human comprehension (9:10). By this summary statement of God's power in nature, Job argued that it was useless for man to believe that he could win his match with God.

In verses 11-13, Job extended his argument to the human realm. Man cannot see God nor detect His passing (9:11). He can only view the ruin about him. Man dares not question His actions (9:12). His "anger" is beyond human control. He allows His wrath to fall when and where He pleases (9:13a). Even the helpers of Rahab, the great and powerful sea monster, are subject to Him (9:13b). Since these dare not contend with God, Job wondered at his doing so (9:14). Should Job call God to the bar of justice?

Were He to answer his summons, Job did not believe that He would give ear to his charge (9:15, 16). In fact, he could only believe that He would come in the whirlwind and but add to his afflictions (9:17). He would leave him "winded" and with increased bitterness (9:18). Should the matter of strength be considered, God's strength would be overwhelming. Should the matter of justice be examined, Job would be denied so much as an appointment (9:19). Job was powerless. Helpless, he was in no position to challenge God. Even if he could, he would be so overwhelmed by God's appearance that, though he knew himself to be innocent, he would declare himself guilty with his own mouth (9:20).

Nevertheless, Job asserted that he was innocent and at the same time recognized that he was disregarding his own welfare because God would react negatively. Yet it no longer seemed to matter to him (9:21). For the moment anyway, it appeared to Job that God would slay the "perfect" with the "wicked" (9:22). The difference which right seemed to have once made, no longer mattered. In fact, Job said, "God mocks at those who have fallen through calamity" (9:23). From Job's standpoint, it looked as though God had forgotten the righteous and had turned them over to judges whose faces were blinded to the differences between right and wrong (9:24a, b). Then in the remainder of verse 24, Job raised a question. He asked his friends to tell him who is responsible for all such conditions if it is not God?

In 9:25-35, Job turned his attention back to his own case. He bemoaned the brevity of life. His days flew by with the speed of the swiftest runner, the fastest ship or the eagle after its prey (9:25, 26). If he should decide to drop his "complaint," to turn from his mourning and become cheerful, he would not follow through because he was afraid he would be faced with some new sorrow since God still considered him guilty (9:27, 28) or at least Job believed that He did. Therefore, why "labor" to prove himself "innocent"? He would be condemned anyway (9:29). Even though he were to scrub himself with the most powerful cleansing agents, God would besmear him with such filth that his garments would be unable to conceal it (9:30, 31).

After expressing such a pessimistic outlook, Job turned back to the original argument of the chapter. He could not appeal to God and expect justice because God is not a man (9:32). Job believed that what was needed was a mediator ("umpire") one who would take the views of God and those of himself and properly arbitrate them, but there was no such person available (9:33). If only God would withhold Job's afflictions and withdraw his terror, then he would present his case without fear because he was not conscious of anything in his own life which should have caused him to be afraid (9:34, 35). He was not afraid of what he would do at the trial; he was afraid of what God would do. If an impartial judge were to be appointed, Job believed he would receive a fair trial. Otherwise, he would continue to be overwhelmed by the very presence of God.

Chapter 10 is an attempt on Job's part to explain all that had happened to him. Still despairing of life, he decided to speak out of the anguish of his soul (10:1). He began by entreating God not to "make" him guilty but to show him why his afflictions had come upon him (10:2). Then he asked if it was profitable for God to "oppress" the righteous, who were the "labor of his hands," and to bless ("shine upon") the plans of the wicked (10:3). God's eyes, Job believed, were not those of a man who sees only as men see (10:4). On the contrary, He sees things as they really are, not as Job's friends had stated. His days and years are not brief like those of a man that he must hasten to judge man, as in Job's case, before he is guilty (10:5, 6). In verse 7, Job charges that God knew he was innocent, yet insisted upon holding him as a guilty person.

Having protested God's treatment, Job continued his argument against Him. He questioned the logic of God's having "fashioned" him for the purpose of destroying him (10:8). He could not understand the reason which would allow or demand that one so carefully "fashioned" be brought to dust again (10:9) after having been created in the womb and allowed to reach manhood (10:11, 12). Since these things had been realized through the generosity of God, Job questioned having been allowed his birth and manhood if all the while God knew it was to be terminated in such a cruel way (10:13). This he could question because he believed it to be a part of God's design from the first to deal severely with him (10:14). Because of his innocence in the midst of his suffering, Job believed that he would have to suffer, whether "wicked" or "righteous," since this was God's purpose for him (10:15). If he even lifted his head, he would be attacked by God who was as relentless as a lion in search of prey (10:16a). For Job, the marvels of creation were offset by the afflictions which he had endured (10:16b). His sufferings, which declared him a sinner, brought host after host — affliction after affliction — to war against him (10:17).

Now, as if in conclusion to his speech, Job returned once more to the question of his birth. It would have been better for him had he never appeared ((10:18). He would prefer to have been taken from his mother's "womb to the grave" (10:19). But this had not happened. Since he had but few days of life left, he entreated God to turn His attention away from him that he might have a short time of relief before he went to the grave (10:20, 21). In light of the grim prospects awaiting him in death, he felt that he deserved a respite. Death held only dark forebodings for him (10:22). Sheol, the abode of the dead, was a domain lacking order or so much as a ray of light. Therefore, Job sought a moment of relief before the bondage and darkness of Sheol lay hold of him.

6. *Zophar's Initial Speech* (11:1-20). After verbal bouts with Eliphaz and Bildad, Job was confronted by his third friend, the orthodox Zophar. As did those before him, he brought Job little comfort. He was authoritarian and severe in his attitude toward all who disagreed with him, especially to those whose thoughts were more profound than his own.

Zophar opened his salvo by suggesting that Job had talked too much. The questions of verses 2 and 3 are phrased so as to suggest that Job's profusion of words did not really reflect the true situation. They were empty and meaningless words. Therefore, it would have been better for him to have remained silent. He had but boasted of his own innocence while guilty and had mocked at the belief that sin inevitably results in suffering. These beliefs, in Zophar's estimation, were heresy.

In verse 4, Zophar offered a summary statement of Job's claims as he saw them. Job, by claiming his theology (doctrine) was not faulty and that he was innocent of the things of which the friends believed him to be guilty, had reflected upon the orthodox theology of his day. This provoked Zophar's severe speech.

Zophar, having heard Job's declaration of the situation as he saw it, expressed his wish that God would speak up and present His side of the case (11:5). After that, Job would see his guilt and experience the profound and manifold wisdom of God which was beyond the comprehension of man (11:16a, b). Job would see that he had been the recipient of far less than he really deserved (11:16c).

Following his introduction to the concept of God's wisdom, Zophar elaborated upon it in 11:7-12. He raised the question as to whether man can fathom the profundity of the wisdom of the "almighty unto perfection" (11:7). That is, man might be able to find God, but can he comprehend fully ("unto perfection") His purpose and its significance? Zophar suggested that he could not. God's purposes are as impossible for man to understand as the scaling of the heavens or the penetration of Sheol (11:8). They are too long and too broad for human comprehension (11:9). If God should pass by this weak creature, man, and seize ("shut up") him as Job charged in 9:11, 12, He could not be hindered from His purpose in the least. Zophar suggested, in light of man's lack of comprehension and the remote possibility of its being improved, that it was possible for him to sin and never be aware of it (11:12). Yet God could see it at first glance (11:11). It was the sin then which *God* saw that brought human suffering. It was not the caprice of God, Zophar argued.

Since suffering, according to Zophar, was the result of sin, Job was counseled to turn to God. By doing so, he would be setting his "heart aright." He should stretch his hands toward God (the posture and sign of prayer), put away sin ("iniquity") and practice only righteousness (11:13, 14). Then, and here he referred back to Job's complaint of 10:15, Job's face would no longer reflect the sign ("spot") of a guilty man but he would be as "steadfast" as a molten statue securely fixed to its base (11:15). The "misery" which Job had known would flow like water from him and leave no evidence of having been there (11:16). The darkness that once covered Job would be banished and light like that of the morning and the noonday, would illuminate his life (11:17). His fears for security and safety would all disappear (11:18). He could lie down without anxiety and those who formerly respected him would again honor and revere him ("make suit unto thee") (11:19). Finally, by way of conclusion, Zophar subtly reminded Job of what happens to the wicked, that is, to those who refuse to turn to God (11:20). By doing so, he was insisting that Job was guilty and, therefore, needed to repent before he could ever be restored to his former state.

7. *Job's Response to Zophar* (12:1 — 14:22). Job reacted to the charges brought against him with increased sarcasm. In his response, he addressed some of his remarks to his three friends (12:2 — 13:19) and the remainder to God (13:20 — 14:22).

Job opened his fourth speech by declaring sarcastically that his friends were "the people," that is, they were the ones with knowledge and that with their passing wisdom would disappear (12:2)!

After his biting opening statement, Job claimed to have known the things Zophar had spoken in 11:7-12. These were things which he and others, as well, had known all along (12:3). Yet his friends instructed him as one who did not know, and by doing so, they grieved him and made him a "laughing-stock" (12:4a). After all, he had called upon God in the past and He had responded. By making that claim, Job was contending that he was "just" and "perfect" and yet was made "a laughing-stock" (12:4b).

In verse 5, Job observes that it is easy for those who are not suffering to lose sight of the possibility of a righteous man suffering. His friends, like others, were ready to refuse sympathy to him or any other sufferer because they saw them as being responsible for their condition (12:5). Even the righteous man, when suffering, was disdained. He was accused of the grossest sins. On the other hand, Job charged that all the while the "righteous" were suffering, the unrighteous continued to live in security and abundance (12:6). This he could not understand.

In the remainder of chapter 12, Job continues to chide his accusers by arguing that their knowledge was not a superior knowledge but that it was a knowledge which anyone, even the creatures, could gain. The whole creation knew that the life of every being was in the hands of God (12:7-10). This could be seen by anyone. It was as natural as taste to the palate or hearing to the ears (12:11).

In verse 12, Job raises the issue of whether "wisdom" and "understanding" may not be with him as well as with the ancients (12:12). After all, Job thought he could know some things. Did he not have ears? Could he not understand? Certainly, Job insisted! Yet his friends had denied him the possibility of having said that wisdom was only with the aged (12:12). But Job would not be outdone. He declared that wisdom is also with God (12:13). He is not only wise, but powerful also. He knows how to accomplish His purpose. He controls the world in which men live (12:14, 15). He can destroy cities, dry up the water or by converse action send them forth to flood the earth as He wills.

Not only did Job acknowledge God's control over the natural realm, he also took note of His sovereignty over men

(12:16-22). This is reflected in the fact that He controls the destiny of all men — the "deceived" and "the deceiver" (12:16). He sets up circumstances which strip "counsellors" of their wisdom and, by the same process, He denies "judges" the ability to make just decisions (12:17). The religious and national leaders are stripped of their roles and the mighty are made weak by Him (12:18, 19). The "trusty" (discreet or able man) is denied his ability to speak and the understanding of the "'elder" is taken away (12:20). "Princes" are held in contempt and the "strong" are rendered incapable (12:21). God uncovers the plots and conspiracies devised by men in darkness (12:22). Nothing is concealed from His eyes. No one can resist His power. Even the nations are subject to His designs. They are increased or destroyed according to His purpose (12:23). Their leaders turn to foolish men who lead astray and they grope about as drunk men without chart or compass (12:24, 25).

Having digressed in the preceding verses, Job turns his attention back in chapter 13 to his criticism of his friends. He begins by claiming that he knows everything they know (13:1, 2). Even so, he had rather debate the issues with God than with them (13:3) because he saw them as makers of false claims (13:4a), as "physicians" who cannot deal satisfactorily with the sickness of the patient (13:4b). This being the case, Job suggests that the wisest role for them would be silence (13:5). Having said that, Job presents the basis for his suggestion.. He charges them with being partial to God to the point of making false claims for Him (13:7, 8). Job believes that God would see through their deception and, rather than reward them, He would reprove them (13:9-11). Then, by way of a conclusion, Job states his belief that the arguments of his friends, which had a long history behind them, would be as useless as "ashes" or soft clay in the building of a defensive wall (13:12). With these words of castigation, Job turns from the friends and fixes his attention upon God once again.

This section begins with Job asking for silence, and insisting upon his own innocence, and he did so in spite of the consequences (13:13). He would take his own "flesh" in his teeth, as an animal would its prey, all the while knowing the risk of losing. Job would nevertheless run whatever risks were involved (13:14). He insisted upon defending himself, even though he realized that there was little hope outside of death (13:15). Yet the very fact that he had the audacity to "come before" God must certainly suggest the possibility that he might be delivered (13:16).

With these words providing the context, Job asked to be heard (13:17) and he did so believing his argument to be sound. He declared, with a degree of confidence, that he would be justified (13:18). He could not conceive of a fair argument resulting in his condemnation (13:19).

Having turned to God, Job asked two things of Him (13:20). He asked for the withdrawal of His hand of affliction and deliverance from fear (13:21). After that, he would serve the role of plaintiff or defender as God chose (13:22) but Job must be shown his sins (13:23). Until then, he could not understand God's hiding His face (treating him so) and dealing with him as an enemy (13:24). After all, Job was as helpless and worthless as a leaf or piece of straw driven by the wind (13:25). Surely God had more important things to do than harass him, he reasoned.

Job then charged God with having written "bitter things," just like a judge writing out a stiff sentence, not because of what he did as a man, but because of what he had done in the immaturity of his youth (13:26). By saying this, Job expressed his belief that God had to search for something to lay to his charge. God had so circumscribed Job that he could not escape His gaze if he wished to do so (13:27) even though he was like a decomposing object or a garment which had been ruined by moths (13:28). In other words, Job could not comprehend God's persistency in afflicting him. After all, there was not much left and that which did remain was weak and decomposing.

In chapter 14, Job turns to describe the condition of man in the world: "Man . . . born of a woman" is weak: his days are limited and filled with trouble (14:1). His life is as transitory as that of a flower and, like a shadow, he is soon gone (14:2). Nevertheless, Job states his belief that God keeps His eye upon man so He can bring him to judgment at the least provocation (14:3); this, though no man is free from all sin ("clean"). If, on the other hand, there should be one, then the judgment would be just (14:4). There being no sinless man, however, Job suggests that God ought to deal with all of them less severely (14:5, 6).

In 14:7-12, Job expresses the belief that the heavens have more possibility of disappearing than he has for living again. If he were a tree, and cut down, he could anticipate the stump sprouting, producing boughs and living again (14:7-9), but with man it was not so (14:10). His hope was as empty as that of an ocean void of water or a dry river bed (14:11). This poor man "lieth down and riseth not" (14:12). There was no hope for him. Yet, Job opens the next paragraph with the wish that it would not be that way.

Job reveals his desire for an after-life by entreating God to leave him in Sheol until His wrath had dissipated, and then to remember him (14:13). How wonderful that would be! "But, could it be?" Job asks himself. With the hope burning in his breast, he phrases the memorable question, "If a man die, shall he live again?" If it could be, then he could live in the assurance that one day he would be relieved of the servitude of death just as a soldier is relieved from his post of duty at the end of his watch (14:14). God would call to him and he would answer (14:15). With these words one is able to see the struggle going on within Job's mind. He was struggling with two Gods. First, the one who had abandoned him because of his sins, and the other, the one who longed for his companionship and whom he hoped would bring him back from Sheol. But he soon turned from the God who would bring him back to the One who had cast him into his affliction.

Turning back to the circumstances at hand, Job described his own sad plight. He complained that God had numbered every wrong step and had taken note of every sinful act (14:16). These He had "sealed up," as though they were

treasures (14:17), until Job could be properly punished. As
a consequence, man's hope was small indeed. If the mountains could be destroyed, how could frail man expect to
escape (14:18, 19)? Just as waters wear stones away, the
judgment wears away any hope man might have. He is
consigned to death (14:20), and he could not expect to
escape because of the persistence of God. His only hope
was the hope he might have had in the accomplishments of
his sons, but he would never know whether they succeeded
or not (14:21). As for man himself, nothing awaits him
but pain and mourning (14:22).

With verse 22, the first cycle of speeches is concluded.
Little did Job realize it, but he was to face even harsher
words from his friends.

FOR FURTHER STUDY

1. Read the articles on "Leviathan" in *IDB*, Volume III,
p. 116 and in *DB*, pp. 578-579.

2. Read the articles on "Angel" in *IDB*, Volume I, pp.
128-134 and "Angels" in *DB*, pp. 32-33. Read the article on
"Angel" in *ZPBD*, p. 39.

Also read pages 289-296 in *The Theology of the Old Testament* by A. B. Davidson.

3. Read the article on "Dream" in *IDB*, Volume I, p. 868
and the one on "Dreams" in *DB*, pp. 221-222.

4. Read the article on "Dead, The Abode of" in *IDB*,
Volume I, pp. 787-788 and the one on "Sheol" in *DB*, p. 906.

5. How do you justify Job's charges against God?

6. What do you see as the implications of Job's desire
to have an umpire to decide the issue between him and
God?

7. What do you see as the main fault of Job's friends? Do
you know anyone with similar theological positions?

CHAPTER 4

CHAPTER 4

The Second Cycle of Speeches

(Job 15 – 21)

1. Eliphaz's Second Address to Job (15:1-35)
2. Job's Response to Eliphaz (16:1 – 17:16)
3. Bildad's Second Address to Job (18:1-21)
4. Job's Response to Bildad (19:1-29)
5. Zophar's Second Address to Job (20:1-29)
6. Job's Response to Zophar (21:1-34)

In the first cycle of speeches, Job's three friends told him that his suffering was punishment for the sins he had committed. Though his sins were obviously unknown to them, on the basis of their theology they presumed he had sinned. In the second cycle, the charges of the friends grew more severe as they attempted to convince Job they were right. As in the first cycle, Eliphaz spoke first.

1. *Eliphaz's Second Address to Job* (15:1-35). Eliphaz, believed to be the oldest, and usually considered the wisest, began his second speech by raising the question of whether wise men are given to use empty, meaningless and profitless words (15:2, 3). He believed that Job's ideas were a hindrance to the faith of others (15:4). He charged him with a knowledge of guilt which he had been seeking to hide

by his own claim that he had done no wrong (15:5) and
stated his conviction that Job's own mouth had condemned
him (15:6).

In verse 7, Eliphaz turned to Job's question, "Who know-
eth not such things as that?" (12:3b), and asked him if he
was the first man to be born or whether he was in existence
before the hills. If so, Eliphaz was interested in knowing
if he (Job) was at the heavenly council that decided on
creation and whether wisdom had been reserved just for
him (15:8). Then, using Job's words (12:3, 9; 13:2), he
asked what knowledge or understanding he had that they
did not possess as well (15:9). After all, they had age and
experience on their side (15:10) and Job should be willing
to accept their wisdom as superior. Claiming divine origin
for their words, Eliphaz asked if they were not consolation
enough for Job (15:11) and, if they were, he wondered why
Job had permitted passion to turn him to anger and rage
(15:12, 13). This in itself proved that Job was but a man.
He could not claim innocence (15:14). Not even the angels
in heaven could pass such a test (15:15). Therefore, man
could never expect to do so (15:16).

Turning from the very pointed comparison of verses 15
and 16, Eliphaz stated that his argument was based upon
the teachings of the fathers and that they were free from any
foreign or pagan elements (15:17-19). Believing his point
had been made, he turns to describe the fate of the wicked.

In verse 20, he states that the wicked man will never
know anything except suffering. He will be haunted by
imaginary horrors – expecting robbery and destruction on
every hand (15:21, 22). Fear will drive him from one disappointment to another (15:23-24) and all because he has
not humbled himself before God (15:25-26). Instead, he
has placed his emphasis upon the physical side of life as
evidenced by his fattened condition which was the result of
extravagant living (15:27). He has rebuilt cities that God
had destroyed, which should have been left in ruins (15:28).
Even so, he will never be rich (15:29). His fruit will be
destroyed (15:30). Consequently, let him not trust in his

own vanity. To do so is sin and the wages of sin is calamity (15:31-33). Every evidence of sinful man shall perish (15:34). In conceiving mischief and bringing forth iniquity, he prepares his own undoing (15:35).

By taking this particular approach, Eliphaz was trying to offset Job's disagreement that all suffering was the result of the individual's sin. Man, according to Eliphaz, is responsible for his destruction. It could never be blamed on the arbitrariness of God. For this reason, Job should be careful with his use of words (compare 15:2, 3).

2. *Job's Response to Eliphaz* (16:1 — 17:16). Job's answer to Eliphaz was in some ways a repetition. He reminded him that he had already heard everything he had said in his second address and if that was all they had to offer, then, they had been miserable comforters (16:1, 2). Their attempts to console Job had but increased his distress. Seeking to minimize what they had said, he turned their words back upon them (compare 8:2; 15:2) by inquiring if there was to be no end to "words of wind," or, if his words had so provoked them (16:3). After all, and it was with scorn on his lips, Job claimed that he, too, could have spoken and acted as they, had they been in his place (16:4). In such an eventuality, he would have spoken words as they, which were from the lips only (16:5) and which would have brought them as little comfort as theirs had brought him.

Following the sarcastic words in 16:1-5, Job called attention to his pathetic situation in spite of his innocence (16:6-17). Even though he cried out, his "pain is not assuaged." On the other hand, if he remained silent, that did not help (16:6). All he held dear was taken from him. He was weary from loss of health, strength, family and friends. They were all gone (16:7). His calamity had laid such a hold on him that he had wasted away (16:8). This, if nothing else, was sufficient evidence of his guilt for his friends, but it could not justify what had happened as far as Job was concerned.

From Job's viewpoint, God had "torn" him as a wild animal tears its prey and had hunted ("persecuted") him that

He might gnash him after He had found him (16:9). But that was not all. Men had joined in the attack and the "unrighteous" were delighted in his state (16:10, 11). He who was once "at ease" and secure in his possessions, was suddenly devastated by one blow after the other (16:12). Job saw himself as God's target. He had been fired upon and left with gaping wounds from which his vitals had spilled out upon the ground (16:13). He was broken down as a wall which had been breached and as one run upon by a mighty man (16:14).

Because of one calamity after the other, Job was dressed in sackcloth (a sign of mourning) and his horn (his strength) was prostrate in the dust (16:15). He had wept until his face was inflamed and his eyes showed signs of approaching death, but without cause (16:16, 17). Such things should have happened to the wicked but not to him, Job insisted. He had not been guilty of violence. There was not the slightest evidence of such when he lifted his hands to God in prayer. They showed no signs of sin.

Following his denial of guilt, Job called upon his heavenly witness to verify his position and, by doing so, to vindicate him (16:18 — 17:9). But, if he were slain, Job hoped that his innocent blood would cry out for justice (16:18). In this way Job appealed to God, but at the same time he appealed against Him (16:19). By doing so he revealed, as before, the inner struggle of dealing with the God whom his friends had presented and God as he believed Him to be. Since his friends, who should have comforted him, had scoffed at him, Job turned to God in the hope that He would take up his cause and argue it with Himself (16:20, 21). Is Job here reaching for the mediator he had lamented in 9:3? If so, the mediator would have been God Himself. That is, God would have mediated Job's cause with Himself. In any case, He would need to decide quickly because time was growing short (16:22). Job's death was imminent (17:1). Yet, his friends continued their provocations (17:2). They should have been more sympathetic and understanding. Instead, they pressed their charge and but added to Job's misery.

Job addresses God again in verse 3. This time he asked Him to make bail for him, with Himself, because He alone could or would do so. Job believed he would ultimately die as a result of what was in process, but he wanted bail so he would have time to go through the procedure which he hoped would vindicate him. By revealing his desire for bail, Job proved that, as far as he was concerned, he had given up all hope of help from his friends. They would never take up his cause. They were without understanding. Therefore, they would never be exalted by seeing their claim verified (17:4). Anyone who denounces a friend, for the price of seeing his claim verified, will see a judgment which will have such a lingering result that it will affect his children (17:5).

God had made Job a "byword" among those who had formerly known and respected him, and he had come to be held in contempt by everyone else (17:6). His resultant weeping had practically blinded him and his body had become a shadow of what it once was (17:7). The upright would be so appalled by this, Job believed, they would be roused "against the godless" (17:8) and even though all was not as it might have been, the righteous should hold on to "his way" because he would grow stronger and stronger for having done so (17:9).

After having slighted his friends by denying that there was a wise man among them, and having called them to attack him again (17:10), Job stated that the days in which he knew joy and accomplishment were now gone (17:11). His friends had suggested that his night was day, that is, that his dread and dark experience was in reality the beginning of day (17:12) but Job would have none of it. He repeated his hope of death because, in that abode, he would be at rest (17:13-16). Though Job had not always felt this way and though he did not know how rest would be accomplished, he believed it would somehow come to pass. In this belief, one can begin to see a development in

Job's thinking. It was evidently the result of the struggle
which he had been having with the God presented by his
friends and God as he knew and understood Him.

3. *Bildad's Second Address* (18:1-21). Job, having reached
a new plateau in his personal struggle with the two views
of God, was once again attacked by one of his friends. This
time Bildad was much more open and deliberate than before. He began by attacking Job for the way he (Job) had
evaluated his friends in his previous speech and for his ex-
pectation that things would be changed just for him (18:1-4).
He insisted that the prosperity ("light") of wicked men will
"be put out" and the flame on his hearth (a sign of security
and peace) will be extinguished (18:5). There will be nothing left for the wicked, not even a light for his tent (18:6).
His walk will no longer be that of a man of wealth, but that of
one in difficult straits, because his counsel (designs) will
have caught up with him (18:7). He will be ensnared in
traps woven by his own evil designs (18:8-10). Haunted on
every hand, fear will hound his every step (18:11). Calamity will always await him with its insatiable hunger (18:12).
A fatal illness will take hold of him and will ultimately take
him from his earthly abode (18:13, 14). Then his dwelling
will pass on to others, after it has been purified (18:15).
Just a few, if any, would be aware the wicked had ever lived.
  Bildad then returned to comparisons made earlier and
stated his belief that the wicked will be like the plant which
has dried up (18:16). They will not have so much as one
son to perpetuate their name (18:17). The light they once
knew will be lost to them and they will be driven from the
face of the earth (18:18). They will leave the world without a survivor (18:19), and for generations to come men will
be astonished and horrified at what had happened to those
who have not known God (18:20, 21).

4. *Job's Response to Bildad* (19:1-29). Job opened his
sixth speech by rejecting the harsh words of his friends.
He charged them with words so cruel they had crushed him

(19:2). So many times had they reproached him that they had lost all awareness of his being a human being (19:3). Then Job raised the issue as to how it could have harmed them if he had sinned (19:4). After all, it would have been a personal matter. Job called to their attention that if what they said was true, then he had been "subverted" and trapped. He was not guilty of the sins with which they had charged him (19:5, 6). Therefore he cried out, but no one heeded him (19:7). Instead, the wall which had hemmed him in was raised higher and the light of the path to deliverance was extinguished (19:8). Job had been stripped of every claim to virtue ("glory") and denied any right to righteousness ("crown") (19:9). As a building reduced to rubble or an unrooted tree, he lay prostrate (19:10). God had turned His wrath loose against him and treated him as an adversary (19:11). God had sent His "armies" against Job and encamped around him as though he dwelt in a fortress when, in reality, he dwelt in nothing but a tent (19:11, 12).

As a result of all that had happened, Job was estranged from family and friends (19:13-15). Even his wife and kin could no longer endure him (19:17, 19). His condition was so bad little children despised him (19:18). He was barely alive (19:20). So, he called upon his friends to open their hearts to him and to leave off their persecution (19:21, 22). He believed he deserved better than this.

In the final paragraph of this reply to Bildad, Job declares his confidence that he will be vindicated. If only his words could be indelibly written that they might survive him, then after his death, if in no other way, he would be vindicated (19:23, 24). But as for himself, it was as though he were already vindicated. He believed that the One to vindicate him would at least appear and, after death, he would see Him, and behold, it would be God (19:25, 26)! God would be on his side rather than appear as a stranger (19:27). Job at last saw a way of deliverance but he had to wait. The very thought of this overwhelmed him (19:27c).

Just before concluding his words in response to Bildad,

he warned his friends of the effect which their insistence upon his guilt would have. Their persistent persecution of him would bring punishment upon them and then they would know about judgment firsthand (19:28, 29). After that, they would understand his problem better. On this sober note Job left off speaking.

5. *Zophar's Second Address to Job* (20:1-29). Zophar broke forth, in his second address, in hot pursuit of Job. He claimed that his thoughts hurried him on to pursue the matter (20:2). He had heard of Job's reproofs and was put to shame; therefore, he had to give a reply (20:3).

Ignoring Job's own situations, and irritated by his defense of himself, Zophar opened his harangue on the brevity of the "triumph" and "joy" of the wicked by declaring that it has always been that way (20:4, 5). His stature, be it ever so lofty, has nothing to do with the outcome (20:6). If he is wicked, he will perish, never to be seen again (20:7-9). Any who might survive would court the favor of the poor by returning what their father had taken from them through dishonest practices (20:10). Those who leave such a trail of woe will have to accomplish it in a short space of time because they will be cut down just at the moment they reach the pinnacle of their success (20:11).

Having delivered himself of the cutting words in verses 4-11, Zophar turns to elaborate upon sin's retribution in the section which follows (12-19). Though one enjoys sin and tries to retain its taste as long as possible, in the end it will poison him and he will not be able to keep it down (20:12-15). The resources accumulated by the wicked prove to be as fatal as the poison of the asp or the viper (20:16). He will not survive long enough to look upon the plenty for which he labored (20:17) and if he does, he cannot hold on to it (20:18). It is the fruit of oppression and violence (20:19) and destined to be lost.

Such wicked men as those described above — and doubtless Zophar placed Job in that category — will never be able to satisfy their greed (20:20). They will devour the weak, until there are none to devour, and that will end their prosperity (20:21). Then, just as they lay hold upon all that is about them, they will find that even they will not be satisfied with it. Their misery will be great, because the tragedy they have brought on every person whom they have disfranchised will recoil upon their own heads (20:22). Just at their most satisfying moment, God's wrath will fall upon them (20:23). If they escape, one weapon after another will smite them and fill them with the terrors of death (20:24, 25). Nothing but darkness will await them and they and their households will be wracked with the fire of disease (fever) (20:26). The heavens and the earth will unite to move against them and will declare their guilt (20:27). All they have accumulated will soon be gone (20:28). These horrible things are the inevitable portion of the wicked. This is what God has assigned to those who live their lives in sin (20:29). Though Zophar's words were directed against the wicked in general, it is obvious that he had Job in mind all the while. With this we await Job's response.

6. *Job's Response to Zophar.* (21:1-34). Job opened his response by asking the undivided attention of his friends. If they would give him their attention and take to heart what he had to say, they would not try to comfort him again (21:2). This would be the end of their consolations and he would be burdened with them no more.

In verse 3, Job turned his full attention to Zophar as seen in the change from the plural to the singular. He asked for the privilege of speaking. Afterwards, Zophar could continue with his mocking as in chapter 20. But before that, Job wished to know why Zophar's reaction had been so severe. Job had not complained against him (21:4); his complaint had been with God. Why, then, should there be a question about his complaining? After all, his condition was so pathetic that men were shocked. When they looked, they were "astonished," covered their mouths and gasped in horhor at his state (21:5). As for Job, just the thought of what was happening was horror enough, but to be the brunt of the affliction was an unbelievable thing indeed (21:6). Therefore, he thought he was justified in his complaint.

In 21:7-16, still troubled by what he believed to be injustice in his own case, Job raised the issue of the prosperity of the wicked. If in such agony death resulted, and without just cause, why then was it that the wicked did not suffer, die young, or lose their influence and power (21:7)? What had happened to Job had not happened to the wicked. Their children had survived and were "before their eyes" because they had been spared the smiting of God ("rod of God") (21:8). They had lived free from fear (21:9a). Their flocks had increased (21:10). Their children, great in number, had lived a life of joy and when their end came, it was swift and without prolonged anguish as in Job's own case (21:11-13). These things Job could not understand. The wicked had rejected God and refused to practice His ways (21:14, 15) and yet they prospered (21:16a). But as for Job, in spite of having refused to follow the advice of the wicked, he had suffered (21:16b). This he could not understand.

Following his discussion of the prosperity of the wicked, Job raised a question over the fact that the godless rarely, if ever, seem to suffer (21:17-22). Bildad had stated that the wicked would be afflicted in 18:5, 12, but Job had seen no signs of it. In verse 17, he asks how often any had seen it happen. How often had anyone seen them driven about like stubble and chaff (21:18)? Even though it had been believed that the fathers' sins would affect the children for generations, Job saw no punishment for the wicked in that (21:19). If the wicked were to be punished, the wrath of God would have to fall on them (21:20). After all, they did not care what happened to their offspring when their own life span was about to be cut short (21:21).

In 21:22, Job went on to condemn his friends for attributing their doctrine of suffering to God. He declared that God is too exalted to be instructed by man on how to respond to a given situation. Leaving the problem of the prosperity of the wicked and their lack of suffering, Job turned to a discussion of death (21:23-26). His observations pointed to the fact that one man dies at the pinnacle of life when all is going well (21:23, 24). Another dies in great suffering and without ever having tasted prosperity (21:25). They are both put into the ground and eaten by the worms (21:26). Therefore, if what the friends have argued is so, it makes no difference whether a man does good or evil. In the end both go the same way.

In 21:27, Job charges that his friends had him in mind all the while as they described the fate of the wicked. They had asked about the dwellings of the princely oppressor and the less exalted wicked man (21:28). Their questions implied that they were no more. But Job suggests that the man in the street be asked for his testimony (21:29). As far as Job was concerned, the evidence was just the opposite to what his friends had claimed. Verse 30 should probably read, "That the evil man is spared in the day of calamity? That they are led away in the day of wrath?" In other words, the wicked will have escaped judgment and no one will have had the courage to face them with their deeds and call them to account (21:31). These wicked men have been borne to their graves in honor and their tombs have been guarded as though they were nobility (21:32). They have been buried in the most beautiful valleys and when men see all these honors, they will be tempted to follow their way because they believe it to be the most profitable way (21:33). In light of this and what he thought to be true, Job charged them with falsehood (21:34).

By doing this, Job was rejecting their inferences that he was a wicked man. He had seen through their presumed subtlety when they talked about the sufferings of the wicked. He now understood, completely, that he had been in their mind all the while. Therefore, nothing they said could be taken seriously. He was not guilty. Their accusations were not valid. Their arguments were full of holes. The evidence was against what they said. Job would accept none of their arguments.

FOR FURTHER STUDY

1. Had you been in the place of Eliphaz would you have charged Job with claiming superior wisdom?

2. Did Eliphaz present a valid argument when he claimed to have tradition on his side? See Job 15:10. What role does tradition play in your belief? In your actions?

3. Do you consider Job's complaint against God in chapter 16 wrong? If so, why? If not, why not? Have you ever been tempted to complain as Job did? What were the circumstances?

4. What advance over Job 9:33 do you see in Job's assurance of vindication as reflected in Job 19:23ff? How do you interpret Job 19:25?

5. Have you ever, as Job did, wondered about the prosperity of the wicked? How do you explain it? What conclusions have you made about it? Discuss.

CHAPTER 5

The Third Cycle of Speeches

(Job 22:1 — 26:14)

1. Eliphaz's Third Speech (22:1-30)
2. Job's Third Response to Eliphaz (23:1 — 24:25)
3. Bildad's Third Speech (25:1-6)
4. Job's Third Response to Bildad (26:1-14)

The third and final cycle of speeches was a virtual contest between Job and Eliphaz. Eliphaz spoke first as he had in the other cycles.

1. *Eliphaz's Third Speech* (22:1-30). Eliphaz began his third speech by stating that the very nature of God does not permit him to gain anything by what man does but, on the other hand, man profits greatly by righteous living (22:2, 3). Since man's conduct does not ultimately affect God, reasoned Eliphaz, what He does to man is for man's own benefit. Therefore, it was unreasonable to argue that God would punish Job for his righteousness (22:4). On this logic, Eliphaz intensified his charge that Job's suffering was the result of his own sin and to make his case, he went so far as to list the sins of which Job must have been guilty. They were, interestingly enough, the sins committed by those who had grown rich and powerful. Job had been rich. Since he

had, it would follow, to Eliphaz's reasoning anyway, that Job must have committed the crimes usually associated with the rich and the powerful.

A list of the sins of which Job must have been guilty now follows. He had taken pledges of the outer garment, the only protection of the poor against the cold, which the law required to be returned each night (Exodus 22:26, 27). He had kept them without any sense of concern (22:6). In addition, according to Eliphaz, he must have withheld water from the thirsty and bread from the hungry (22:7). After all, how else could Job's affliction be explained?

Job must have secured his strength and influence by unjust means as did those described by Isaiah in 5:8 (22:8). He had no doubt sent the widow away without his help and the orphan he had left in a pathetic state (22:9). For these reasons, Eliphaz believed, Job had been brought to his terrible state (22:10, 11).

After the charges listed above, Eliphaz sought to straighten out Job's theology. He began by acknowledging the loftiness of God, but he would not accept the charge that he had not become involved with man (22:12). Yet Job had not said that. He had only asked God to turn His gaze away and not look upon him (7:19). Evidently, Eliphaz interpreted it as being something other than what Job had meant (23:13, 14).

In verse 15, Eliphaz asks Job if he would persist in keeping the ways which the wicked of all ages had kept. If so, he, as they, would be snatched away (22:16). Those who turn God away, asking what He could do for them seeing that their houses were already filled with good things, would lose all they had accumulated (22:17-20) and the innocent would mock at their downfall even though they insisted that they had rejected the counsel of the wicked.

As a conclusion to his final address, Eliphaz called on Job to repent and assured him if he should, he would be restored to his former state (22:21-30). He began these words of assurance by encouraging Job to become "acquainted with God" or perhaps, as was more likely, "yield to God," and he would receive the reward of his increase (22:21). Later, having claimed to be the mouthpiece for God, he called on Job to accept his instruction and take it to heart (22:22). If only Job would leave unrighteousness, forsake his desire for treasures and turn to God, he would find greater treasure in Him (22:23-26). Then, whenever Job called upon God, He would hear him and, because of His bountiful goodness, he would always have an occasion to pay the vows he had made to God (22:27). Too, all that Job decreed or wished would come to pass (22:28). When men humbled Job, he would be restored to his former state (22:29) and even when Job prayed for the guilty (Job himself?) they would be delivered on account of his character (22:30). With these generous promises Eliphaz concluded what he had to say to Job. He had not changed from his initial position. If anything, he had grown more severe in his approach.

2. *Job's Response to Eliphaz* (23:1 – 24:25). Ignoring Eliphaz, Job bewailed his undeserved affliction. He began by characterizing his sufferings as being greater than his groanings had indicated (23:2). If only he could find God and face Him with his case, then He would listen, accept Job's argument and acquit him (23:3-7). What bright prospects! But Job could not find Him (23:8, 9). Nevertheless, God knew all about Job and when He tried him he would come out as refined gold (23:10) because he had remained in the way of God (23:11). He had kept His commandments and had held His words to be more essential than food (23:12). Yet, whatever he did, Job believed that God's purpose would be realized, regardless of his claim one way or the other (23:13, 14). The very knowledge of this and the belief that the darkness which engulfed him was from God, whom he could not find, brought terror to Job's heart and reduced his state to one of despair (23:17).

After this defense of his integrity, Job turned to raise some questions about what he believed to be God's indifference to wickedness in the world (24:1-17). He began by wondering why God did not have fixed times to judge the wicked so the righteous would know beyond question that the wicked had received their dues (24:1). They had taken away the lands and flocks of others (24:2-4) and some of those who had been dispossessed themselves had been driven to the desert and had become particularly cruel in taking care of their own needs as well as those of their children (24:5). Those who had been dispossessed, and as a result had become wicked themselves, were driven to the "provender" of cattle for foods and to the despoiling of the vineyards of the wicked ("rich") (24:6). The poor and hungry were without dwellings and their clothing was not enough to keep them warm (24:7, 8).

Though verse 9 is questioned by a number of Old Testament scholars, it could refer to the heartless creditor who had taken the child from its mother's arm as payment on a debt and who had been insensitive enough to refuse the poor their pledge garments as protection against the cold. These disfranchised men and women went about improperly clothed and were treated as slaves, which no doubt many had become, and perished while in the process of harvesting and storing the crops of the wealthy (24:10, 11). Such poor men had cried out in their distress, but they had been ignored by God (24:12).

In 24:13ff., Job turns his attention upon another aspect of life: the wickedness of murder, adultery and housebreaking. Those who practiced these misdeeds did so under the darkness of night (24:13). The first to be dealt with was the murderer. He would rise "before," not "with" the light, slay the helpless and roam the streets in darkness like a thief (24:14). The adulterer, having put a veil over his face, slips in and out without being detected (24:15). Thieves tunnel into the treasuries of men under the cloak of darkness to steal and then hide out during the day (24:16, 17).

Variously treated by scholars, verses 18-21 are believed by some to be an interpolation which modified Job's claim of God's inactivity in face of wickedness. The section begins with a characterization of the wicked. They are depicted as being borne away as vessels upon the water. Their property which had been cursed is no longer frequented by them since it produces no fruit (24:18). These wicked persons are carried down into Sheol as surely as waters are consumed by drought and heat (24:19). They are soon forgotten in the very places where they once held sway (24:20) and it is all because of their cruelty and inhumanity (24:21).

Though verses 18-21 are questioned by some, as suggested above, it is believed by others that the remainder of the chapter consists of Job's words. If so, he is still dealing with the sins of the strong and powerful. He tells of their recovery from what appeared to be fatal illnesses and God's keeping His eyes upon them to keep them safe while in the end they, like all others, were cut down without any distinction having been made as to their wickedness (24:24). So certain was Job of his interpretation of events, that he challenged anyone to prove him "a liar" (24:25). Having spoken these words, he left off his response to Eliphaz, who had been his most severe critic.

3. *Bildad's Third Speech* (25:1-6). Though the arrangement of chapters 25-31 is questioned by numerous scholars, the problem is too complicated to be dealt with in this brief study. Therefore, the headings usually given in the English texts will be followed. In that case, the speech of Bildad consists of only five short verses in which he sought to turn Job's attention to the exalted and matchless power of God. He characterized him as being over the entire universe (25:2). His "armies'" (angels) are without number and the light of His presence enables Him to detect the most secluded spots (25:3). This being so, and since God knows everything, how could man presume to be blameless in God's sight (25:4)? Not even the moon nor the stars could make such claims (25:5); how then could man, who by comparison was no more than a worm (25:6)?

By raising these issues, Bildad had registered amazement at Job's charges of inequity in the world. He asked Job to consider God as He really is and he would see that there can be no injustice in Him. With this said the speeches of the friends come to a close.

4. *Job's Third Response to Bildad* (26:1-14). Job opened his third speech with sarcasm. With biting words, he exclaimed that Bildad's speech had really "helped him" (26:4). In fact, he would have liked to know the source of his great inspiration (26:4). Then he would be able to evaluate it.

The remainder of chapter 26 (5-14) is a description of God's dominion. It is assigned to Bildad by many. In that case, 26:1-4 and 27:1-6 remain for Job. But agreement on this matter is lacking and the nature of the problem is again too complicated for the space available here. Yet, if this section is left with Job's final speech to Bildad, and it may have been, then it is Job who pressed the point of God's dominion and asserted that it reaches even to the abode of the dead (26:5). Sheol and Abaddon (another name for Sheol) are uncovered before His eyes (26:6). Nothing is concealed from His searching. He stretches out the northern lands — all the earth in fact — without support from beneath (26:7). He puts the waters in the clouds as the traveler places them in a water skin (26:8). He conceals His throne that no man may look on Him (26:9). The oceans have their bounds as well as light and darkness (26:10). At His voice (the thunder) the "pillars of heaven" (probably a reference to the mountains) tremble and are terrified (26:11). With His power He "stills" the sea and overpowers the great sea-monster, Rahab (26:12). By His breath He blows the clouds away that the beauty of the heavens may be seen. With His hand He pierces the fleeing serpent (Leviathan?) (26:13). As marvelous as all of this appears to be, it is but a small part of God's work in the universe (26:14a, b). Man cannot comprehend this. How could he ever expect to comprehend the fullness of His work (26:14c)? God's power is beyond finding out.

These words having been spoken, the speech cycle was concluded. To be sure, many suggest that 27:1-6 is a part of Job's answer to Bildad and 27:7-12; 24:18-24; 27:13-23 contain the third speech of Zophar. Even though these suggestions have sufficient basis for some, others believe that Bildad's brevity in the third speech and the lack of a third speech by Zophar indicate that the friends had exhausted their argument and the trailing off into silence was the result. Certainly this position seems tenable. Yet unanimity is lacking.

FOR FURTHER STUDY

1. Eliphaz reasoned that God was not affected one way or the other by man's actions. What is wrong with what he said? What is your evidence to the contrary? Is there any sense in which he may have been right?

2. Are the rich and powerful, as suggested by Eliphaz, more given to sin than the poor and the weak? What evidence has been brought to bear upon your answer? What are the dangers inherent in belonging to either group?

3. Did Eliphaz have any right to promise Job anything, as he did in 22:21-30, in return for his repentance? Do you always expect something in return for everything you do in the will of God? If not, why not? If so, why?

4. For a discussion of the various positions held on the arrangement of chapters 25 – 31 see any reputable commentary on the book of Job.

5. What is your reaction to Bildad's evaluation of man in 25:6? Do you believe it to be a valid attitude? Why? If not, why not?

6. How do you reconcile Bildad's attitude toward man (and certainly he included Job when he spoke of man) and God's attitude as reflected in the prologue?

7. Read the article on "Rahab (Dragon)" in *IDB*, Volume IV, p. 6.

CHAPTER 6
Job's Monologues
(Job 27:1 — 31:40)

1. The Hopelessness of the Godless (27:1-23)
2. A Monologue on Wisdom (28:1-28)
3. Job's Reflections Upon the Past (29:1-25)
4. Job's Reflections Upon the Present (30:1-31)
5. Job's Final Claim of Innocence (31:1-40)

If the arrangement of the material in this section of the book is correct, then, after Zophar's failure to speak a third time, Job took up where he left off speaking to Bildad and, as in the other two cycles, challenged the arguments which had been given. For instance, he had been charged with great wickedness by Eliphaz in his third speech, but in chapter 27 Job challenged this and declared himself innocent. This is especially clear in 27:1-6.

Many believe that the remainder of chapter 27 (verses 7-23) contains Zophar's speech in which he depicted the hopeless condition of the wicked. If this is the case, then the claim that the friends had exhausted their argument for all practical purposes with Eliphaz's third speech may not be quite as convincing as some have held. Yet the matter *could* in the end turn upon what many believe to be a contradiction between Job's attitude expressed in other parts of the book

and that expressed here in 27:7-23. Does Job contradict himself, if indeed these verses are by him, in this section? It
depends upon the identity of the wicked. Is Job talking
about the wicked in general or is he referring, at least in part,
to those who have called him wicked? If the latter is the
case, and there is much to commend it, then this section may
well have been spoken by Job. The following discussion is
based upon that assumption.

1. *The Hopelessness of the Godless* (27:1-23). Chapter
27 begins with Job's insistence upon his innocence. He
opened with an oath and declared that he had been speaking
the truth, which was that God had taken away his claim
("right") to innocence by an affliction which had "vexed"
his deepest being (27:2, 4). In doing so, God had preju-
diced Job's claim of innocence in the eyes of his friends. But
Job insisted while he had all his faculties (27:3), what he
had said was true. It was as though he were saying, with all
his faculties present, that everything which he had said and
was about to say was true. In other words, he had not mis-
represented anything. His lips had been righteous and his
tongue had not spoken deceit (27:4).

In light of Job's insistence that he had been honest in pre-
senting his case, he would never abandon his claim of innocence and verify ("justify") the charges pointedly made in
chapter 22, that he was an unrighteous man (27:5). Job had
not done as his friends had charged and could not understand their insistence upon his repenting of sins which he
had never committed. He insisted upon holding to his innocence (27:6a), but in doing so, he was not claiming that he
had never done wrong That was another matter entirely.
But as far as his denial of the charges of his friends was concerned, he had done so without the slightest fear of reproach
by his conscience (27:6b).

The emphasis changed with verse 7 from Job's claim of
innocence to a description of the godless. If the reference to
the "wicked" was to the wicked in general, as many believe,
then there would seem to be some basis for attributing these

words to Zophar. But if the reference was to Job's friends who rise up as his enemies and accuse him, they may well be the words of Job. Assuming the latter possibility, the remainder of chapter 27 would be Job's vivid description of the hopelessness of the godless. It would not, in that case, be either a condemnation of himself or an admission of guilt. It would simply be a wish on Job's part that those who had charged him ("that riseth up against him") would be treated as the godless (27:7, 8). In that case, the words which follow are but an elaboration upon the hopelessness of such wicked men.

The hopelessness of the wicked is described three ways. First, when "God cutteth off" and "draweth out his soul," that is, at the time of death, he is without hope (27:8); second, he is without hope when trouble overtakes him (27:9); and third, hope is lacking because, as the question implies, he does not "delight himself in the Almighty" or call upon him continuously (27:10). If the words are Job's, and the plural "you" suggests that the address was to the friends and not to Job, he had simply revealed his intention of showing his comforters God's way of dealing with those who defy and deny Him (27:11). In fact, verse 12 suggests that Job believed his friends had seen his ways and, in light of their having done so, he could not understand why they had argued against him in such a cruel way.

As a result of the assumption made at the beginning of this discussion, the last paragraph of chapter 27 must be understood as reflecting Job's own inner struggle. To be sure, the wicked would suffer, as outlined in verses 13-23, but how could this be the explanation of Job's great suffering? He was not guilty of those things with which he had been charged and which were generally believed to bring the kind of suffering outlined here. This, too, was part of the monologue in which he debated the issues before him.

The judgment of the wicked was described in three ways. First, his descendants will be slain by the sword, by famine and pestilence (27:13-15). Second, their accumulations of the years will pass from their hands into the hands of the righteous ("innocent") who will survive them (27:16-18). Finally, the wicked themselves will be taken away as in a great storm and men will mock and hiss at them or possibly at their memory (27:19-23).

2. *A Monologue on Wisdom* (28:1-28). Though often denied as having its source in Job, this chapter is still considered by some to be a continuation of his struggle. If so, it represents an attempt to gain wisdom. If that could happen, then Job would be able to explain to himself the mystery of what had taken place and had to that point remained hidden from his understanding.

Chapter 28 opens with a discussion of man's skill at acquiring the riches of the earth. Since silver, gold, iron and copper have their source in the earth, men seek an end to darkness with a miner's lamp and explore the caverns and man-made shafts of the earth to discover these treasures in order that they might bring them to the surface (28:1-6). The shafts from which they are taken are hidden from the birds (28:7). The beasts of the earth, who are unafraid of the dark, have not even walked there (28:8). Yet man has not been deterred in his search for these valuables. He digs through flint and opens passages through the rocks that these treasures might be uncovered before his eyes (28:9, 10). If the shaft is threatened, and water is referred to as a threat, then the flow is stopped that the treasure may not be lost (28:11). Man will go to any lengths to lay hold upon these treasures. He digs in the earth because it is there that the treasures are found. But what about wisdom? Where is it to be found?

If these words are Job's, the question of wisdom is one that has to do with the knowledge of those factors which control and direct God's purposes in the world — especially those purposes as they relate to the lives of men. What a treasure that would be! Was Job here following through on a belief that there was something yet unknown about his situation? Was there knowledge that Job did not have which would explain what appeared to be a contradiction in God's

dealings with man? Could he come into possession of it?
Perhaps this was what was involved, but where would such
wisdom be discovered (28:12)? It could not be found like
treasure in the earth (28:13) nor gathered from the depths
of the sea (28:14). It could not be bought because it was
above the price of earthly treasures (28:15-19). How then
could such wisdom be acquired? Since it was hidden from
the eye of man and since the nether world had only heard
of it by way of rumor, Job wondered whether it had been
acquired at all (28:20-22).

In verses 23-28, it is clearly stated that understanding,
hidden from man and creature, was the possession of the
Creator. He knows the way "thereto." He is, in fact, its
possessor. Therefore, He is the Creator. In creation the Creator saw wisdom, recounted wisdom, established wisdom,
and then, explored it (28:27). As far as man was concerned
from the beginning, God had declared that wisdom was to
fear Him — hold in reverent awe — and depart or refrain
from evil (28:28). In other words, the wise man is one who
fears God and turns from evil. Was Job claiming such wisdom for himself? Perhaps he was, but whether he was or
not, it must be kept in mind that God had attributed it to
him (see 1:8).

3. *Job's Reflections Upon the Past* (29:1-25). Forgetting
for a moment his own condition and the miserable comfort
of his friends, Job turned his attention to the way things
had been with him in the past and manifested a longing
for a return to those days when God stood watch over him
(29:2), when the radiance and light of his presence had
brought blessings untold (29:3, 4). His fellowship with
God and that of his children had been the greatest sources
of his happiness (29:5). During those days his life had
been filled with an abundance of good things. His steps
"were washed with butter," and the barren rocks produced
rivers of oil (29:6). Both of the images in verse 6 are hyper-
boles which describe the bountifulness of nature toward him.
In those good old days, when he went to the gate of the

city to take his place along with the others who were responsible for governing and deciding issues, the young, out of
respect for him, had stepped out of his path and the aged
had stood to their feet upon his arrival (29:7, 8). As Job
entered their presence, even princes and nobles had remained silent until after he had spoken (29:9, 10). When
men saw him or heard him they had called him blessed
and had spoken with approval (29:11) because in contrast
to what Eliphaz had said of Job in chapter 22, he had
cared for the poor, the fatherless, the perishing and the
widow (29:12, 13). He had been so faithful in his acts of
kindness that righteousness and justice fitted him as appro-
priately as a robe and headdress (29:14). They were natural
and right for him.

When blind men came to him he had become their eyes
and when the lame appeared he became their feet (29:15).
Whatever the need, he made certain it was met (29:16)
even to the point of breaking the power of the oppressor
(29:17).

As a result of all these things, Job had anticipated living
to be an old man and then dying in the midst of his children
(29:18). As a tree planted by the waters and as a field re-
freshed by the heavy dew of night he had found all his
needs met (29:19). It appeared that the respect which men
had felt for him would never diminish nor would his strength
("bow") ever be dissipated (29:20). Men had waited for his
counsel and when he spoke, issues were settled (29:21, 22).
His opinions had been as desirable as rain upon the dry
land (29:23). When he smiled, and his countenance was
always lifted up, the depressed had taken heart (29:24).
As their friend, he had sat among them as their leader.
When he pointed a direction they had followed without
question (29:25). Thus it was obvious that Job had enjoyed
a place of unparalleled influence and prestige, but now all
of that had changed. The present situation was quite
different.

4. *Job's Reflections Upon the Present* (30:1-31). Job's
position in life had been drastically altered by the develop-
ments of more recent times. Whereas he had been held in
honor, he was now mocked by ordinary men, the offspring
of those whom he had refused to hire to tend his flocks
(30:1). They had dissipated their strength and were prema-
turely old (30:2). Because of their impoverished condition
they had wasted away (30:3). Their food consisted of whatever they could scavenge (30:4). As a result of their condition and appearance, they were driven into the wastelands
where they wandered about in search of food and lived like
the wild animals (30:5-8). Such outcasts as these mocked
Job. How pathetic the picture! How drastic the change!

Job, who had been the most respected man of all, had
become a byword for all sorts of men and the subject of
their mocking songs (30:9). They held him in contempt
and demonstrated their disdain for him by spitting when
they saw him (30:10). The reason for this lack of respect
("cast off the bridle before me"), according to Job, was the
way God had afflicted him (30:11). Because of this, he
was an outcast and had been threatened time after time
by this rabble — the offspring of these unworthy men — and
there seemed to be no one willing to take up his cause
(30:12-15).

The plight in which Job found himself had reduced him
to despondency (30:16). His nights were filled with pain
comparable to the piercing of a bone or the tearing of a
limb from the body (30:17). Darkness was a terror for him.
His condition had left him so emaciated that his garment
no longer fitted ("is disfigured"). It draped over him as
loosely as the collar of a tunic (30:18). God had, by bringing this great affliction upon Job, cast him into the mire as
though he were ashes or dust (30:19). Though Job cried
out unto God, the only response was a silent stare (30:20).
God had become his persecutor (30:21). It was as if Job
had been buffeted and would finally be destroyed in the
storm (30:22). He believed that his sufferings could but
lead, finally, to the grave ("the house of meeting") (30:23).

Job seemed convinced that his destiny was already determined. Nevertheless, as a kind of natural reflex or instinct, just as one puts out his hand to break a fall, Job cried out to God for help (30:24). After all, he had wept for others in trouble or in need (30:25). And because of this he would expect the same rewards for himself. But to his dismay, only suffering and darkness came instead (30:26). His afflictions had brought such inner turmoil that his appearance had been distorted (30:27). His skin was blackened, not by the sun, but by the terrible disease which had filled his bones with fever and caused him to cry out like the jackal and ostrich (30:28-30). Little wonder then, that the music of his life had been replaced with sounds of mourning and weeping (30:31).

5. *Job's Final Claim of Innocence* (31:1-40). Having compared the past with the present, in this chapter Job reasserted his claim of innocence and issued his final statement concerning his integrity. He began by declaring that he had "made a covenant" or a pledge with his eyes that they would not look lustfully (31:1) and gave as his reason for doing so the fact that God brings disaster upon those who give way to such practices (31:2-4). Then he continued by asking to be carefully weighed and evaluated. If it should appear that he had followed falsehood and deceit or if he had turned from the way of integrity, then he would accept the fact that he was as one who had sowed but was not worthy of the harvest (31:5-8). By this he meant that if declared to be holding to a false claim, he would be worthy of the denial of the fruits of his labor.

In the second paragraph of the chapter, Job repudiates any charge of immorality. To emphasize his innocence, he formulates a hypothetical case in which, if guilty, he would deserve to lose his wife to another (31:9, 10). His wife would be the concubine of her new master. This was a heinous crime in Israel and deserving of the severest punishment (31:11). It merited complete devastation for the guilty — devastation of his possessions, offspring and person (31:12).

Having held to his personal integrity by his unusual defense in 31:9-12, Job continued his claim of innocence by repudiating any possible charges of the use of abusive power. He began by denying that he had abused his servants when they had come before him to complain (31:13). He believed himself accountable to God for his attitude toward those who served him. If he had abused them, he wondered how he would have been able to justify such actions had God risen up to judge him (31:14). After all, they had been created by the same One who had created him (31:15). In light of that, he would not mistreat a fellow being. He had not, in fact.

When the poor came to him, rather than acting as Eliphaz had charged, Job had cared for them. None of those looking to him for help had been declined (31:16, 17). This had been Job's way from his youth. He had always been like a father to the orphan and a counselor to the widow (31:18). If he had failed to clothe the naked with the best of clothing or if he had taken advantage of his position in the gate to disfranchise, or strike the fatherless, then he hoped God would smite him (31:19-22). If guilty of the latter, and he was no doubt using the shoulder and arm in a figurative sense, then he called for a terrible amputation of the limb involved (31:22). The very possibility of such punishment had served its purpose by having restrained Job from any such action (31:23).

Not only did Job claim fair treatment of those in inferior positions, a thing which all men could readily see, he denied that he had been guilty of secret sins. He rejected Eliphaz's implied charge (22:24ff.) that his greatest joy, hope and trust were in his wealth (31:24, 25) or that he had ever been tempted to worship the sun or moon (31:26). In fact, he went beyond a denial and stated that he had never even been tempted to throw these heavenly bodies a kiss of devotion (31:27). Had he done so, he would have been placing himself in a position of a capital offense (see Deuteronomy 17:2ff.) as well as denying that his God was the Creator (31:28). These things he had never done. Neither had he ever rejoiced over the destruction of his enemies (31:29, 30). No man had ever been turned away from his door hungry or without lodging (31:31, 32). Neither had Job sought, like Adam, to hide his sin (31:33, 34). There had been nothing to hide.

The concluding words of the soliloquy contain, in the first part, an appeal from Job for a list of the specific charges brought against him (31:35). If such were available, he would place it upon his shoulder or wear it as a diadem (31:36). By this response, he stated his belief that the indictment would contain nothing which would reflect upon him. With the indictment in hand, Job would approach God, even after recounting every step or act of his life, and would do it with the assurance of a nobleman, because he was confident that there could be no valid charge (31:37).

The second part of the conclusion to the soliloquy takes up, for the last time, Job's theme of protest. He calls for a curse to fall upon all his fields if they had become his through unjust dealings or at the cost of the lives of their former owners (31:38-40). He was able to do this because of the certainty of his innocence. With this final word of assurance, Job ceases speaking.

For Further Study

1. Do you consider Job's claim of innocence justified? Did he overstate his case? If not, what support outside of his own claim did he have?

2. Read the articles on "Wisdom" in *IDB*, Volume IV, pp. 852-860 and in *DB*, pp. 1039-1040.

3. Read the article on "Elder in the Old Testament" in *IDB*, Volume II, pp. 72-73 and the one entitled "Elder (in OT)" in *DB*, p. 238.

4. Do men still judge others on the basis of their circumstances as men did Job? Is this fair and just? Why not? What great principle is involved in such practices?

5. What was Job's attitude toward others? How did he

treat his own servants? Do you think he would have accused
his friends as they accused him given the same set of
circumstances?

CHAPTER 7

The Elihu Speeches

(Job 32:1 — 37:24)

1. Elihu's Contention That God Speaks to Man (32:1 — 33:33)
2. Elihu's Effort to Vindicate the Justice of God (34:1-37)
3. Elihu's Claim That Righteousness Makes a Difference (35:1-16)
4. Elihu's Argument That God's Ways Are Not Past Finding Out (36:1 — 37:24)

Elihu, a bystander during the debates between Job and his three friends, is now introduced. He delivered four speeches while Job waited in silence. Many scholars believe that the speeches delivered by Eliphaz could be omitted from the book without appreciably affecting the story. Others hold that Elihu's apparent knowledge of the debate and the climax to which he carried it are sufficient reason to retain them as a part of the book. This has been challenged, however, for the reason that Job, according to the Prologue, was not afflicted on account of sin but for the purpose of vindicating God's claims about him. Yet, after a more careful reading, it becomes apparent that the speeches do, indeed, give another dimension to the book. They suggest that suffering has a disciplinary value. This was a new emphasis in the book, but a very important one. Though the book may have served its purpose without these speeches, and as already suggested, some would have it so, they do broaden the base of Job's quest. Therefore, the position that the speeches belong to the original author and serve an important place in a consideration of Job's dilemma seems quite tenable.

1. *Elihu's Contention That God Speaks to Man* (32:1 – 33:33). Elihu's initial speech was preceded by a statement of the reason for the cessation of Eliphaz, Bildad and Zophar and an introduction to Elihu (32:1-5). The name Elihu ("my God is he") also occurs in 1 Samuel 1:1 and 1 Chronicles 12:20; 26:7 and 27:18. But the Elihu of the book of Job was the son of Barachel, a Buzite. According to Genesis 22:21, Buz was the brother of Uz. This probably suggests that Elihu and Job had come from the same region; if so, they may have been related in some way.

There were two reasons given for Elihu's becoming involved in the debate. First, he was incensed by Job's justification of himself and his resultant charges against God (32:2b). Second, he was outraged over the inability of Job's friends to indict him. Even though this appears to be the message of verse 3, there is a tradition which holds that the text originally read so as to effect the condemnation of God rather than Job. In that case, the meaning would have been that the inability of the friends to fix a charge against Job had left God undelivered of Job's charges. But this view is questionable and the former position is to be preferred.

According to verse 4, Elihu had refrained from speaking because of his youthfulness. He had remained in the background until those older than himself had finished their addresses, but he could not remain quiet any longer. To leave Job without an adequate reason or explanation for his condition was more than he could endure (32:5).

Elihu opened his first address with an explanation of why he had not spoken sooner. He claimed that he had refrained from speaking out of deference to age and because of his youthful timidity (32:7). Yet the wisdom of years had not helped in Job's case. Years of experience had been unable to handle his problem. Therefore, Elihu was prompted to express his conviction that wisdom depends upon the "spirit" or "breath of the Almighty" (32:8). According to the implications of Elihu, he (Elihu) was the possessor of this kind of wisdom, not the men of age and experience (32:9).

Out of all those present, Elihu claimed to possess the "spirit" or "breath of the Almighty" and, because of that, he asked to be heard (32:10). He had waited for the "words" and "reasonings" of the three friends to confute Job but to no avail (32:11, 12). Instead, the friends had, upon encountering Job's reasonings, found a case which they could not satisfactorily explain. Only God could handle Job's case (32:13). Yet, Elihu made bold to claim that he had arguments which Job would be unable to refute and they would be quite different from those which the friends had used (32:14).

Turning from his consideration of what the three had failed to do, Elihu reflected upon the scene before him. The friends had nothing left to say (32:15) but should he remain silent because they had been silenced (32:16)? He reasoned that he should not. Instead he would show his opinion ("wisdom"). He could no longer restrain the explosion of words which the spirit had now produced within him (32:17). He was under a duress as formidable as the pressure of wine in an unvented wineskin (32:18, 19). So, he would speak and by doing so, he would find relief (32:20). When he did speak, he would be impartial because he was afraid his "Maker" would dispose of him, without his having accomplished the purpose of his existence, if he were to show partiality (32:21, 22).

Finally, after his boastful introduction and challenge to Job's friends, Elihu turned to Job. He asked him to listen carefully and respond as he was able (33:1). Then, following a claim to sincerity (33:2, 3) he acknowledged that he, like Job, had been created by God. They were of the same stuff and there was no reason for Job to be afraid (33:4-7). Through these words Elihu was claiming his ability to han-

dle Job's difficulty. His case was not as the friends had
suggested in 32:13, but he knew what the problem was and
he would dispose of Job's case in short order. After this
wordy introduction, he finally began.

Elihu opened his case by discussing Job's innocence and
his charge of God's abuse which he had heard with his own
ears (33:8-11). He emphatically stated that God had not
reacted as Job had charged (33:12). He was above such
pettiness. This might be the approach of man, but it would
never be for God because He was morally higher than
man. He would never respond with such arbitrariness.
These traits were too human to be divine.

Following his refutation of any implication of arbitrariness on God's part, Elihu insisted that rather than remaining silent as it may have appeared to Job, God did indeed
speak to man (33:13, 14). He claimed that He had spoken
to him through the dreams which He caused him to have
in the night (33:15). These dreams teach man the truth
about himself and serve to lead him away from destructive
purposes to humility (33:16, 17). This response on God's
part was to keep man from the terrors of death (33:18).

A second way in which God speaks to man is through
the angels. Just when the death angels ("destroyers") lay
hold of man in his weakened condition, another angel, whose
responsibility it is to explain the reason for his suffering,
appears to show man what is right for him (33:19-23). If
he responds favorably, the angel will intercede and ransom
him from the hands of the death angels (33:24). Then, the
sick man regains his health (33:25) and is restored to righteousness as well as to the favor and presence of God (33:26).
Finally, after seeing himself as he really is, he declares that
God has not dealt with him as he had deserved but has,
instead, redeemed him from death and given him the light
of life (33:27, 28).

In the last paragraph of his first speech, Elihu concludes
with a summary statement of God's purpose for speaking
to man (33:24-33). He does it to save him from death and
to give him the light of the living (33:29, 30). Because of

that, Elihu called upon Job to listen while he continued
(33:31), and if he had anything to say, he should say it because Elihu's only wish was that Job be declared righteous
(33:32). If Job had nothing to say, and he could not believe
that he did, then he would proceed to enlighten him further
(33:33).

2. *Elihu's Effort to Vindicate the Justice of God* (34:1-
37). In his second speech to Job, Elihu sets himself to the
defense of God. That He should have been charged with
injustice was beyond his comprehension. As far as Elihu
was concerned, the only injustice associated with God was
the injustice done Himself in His generous dealings with
man.

Turning to those standing about, Elihu admonished the
wise among them to listen (34:2) and to try his words
with the inner ear, that is, to test them as one tests food
with the tongue (34:3). After that, they were to make their
judgments (34:4). Job had made the claim that he had right
on his side and that God had treated him unjustly (34:5).
Yet that which had happened to Job seemed to contradict
his claims (34:6). Elihu asked if there had been another
like Job. He wished to know if there were any others who
would say that virtue was without merit, as Job had, while
at the same time holding on to it with unrelenting tenacity
(34:7). There being no response, Elihu charged Job with
having taken up company with the wicked (34:8). Though
there are no accounts that Job had actually said the things
with which he was charged in 34:9, they could be inferred
from what he had said. In light of these inferences, Elihu
decided to come to God's rescue.

Elihu began his vindication speech by declaring that it
was impossible for God to do wrong (34:10). He argued
that God renders to man what he deserves (34:11) and that
He will never do any more or less than that (34:12). After
all, God had 'not been authorized to take up His position
of authority over the earth (33:13). He had come by it
through His own omnipotence and He was therefore ac-

countable to no one. But if God should only think of Himself and forget man, man would immediately perish (34:14,
15). Therefore, if any injustice had been involved, God had
been unjust to Himself; but that man continued to live
suggests that He was willing to leave it that way. On the
other hand, if He had been unjust in the world, men would
have wanted to condemn Him (34:16, 17). Yet they would
not dare do so because His authority was above that of
earthly rulers (34:18) and He could treat them all alike
because they were His creation (34:19). Proof that He
treats them impartially is to be seen in the fact that He
takes away, without hand (without human help), the strong
as well as the weak (34:20). When men are taken away,
it is because God has beheld in their works some evil deed
(34:21). This was just the opposite of what Job had claimed.
He believed that if God were to look upon him, He would
see that he was not guilty of evil (10:7). Elihu persisted,
however, with his point by stating that there was no place
for man to hide his iniquity (34:22).

Since evil does not escape God, there is no need for Him
to investigate man any further (34:23). There are no inqui-
sitions where the case has to be argued (34:24). In fact,
there is no need for them. God, armed with His infinite
knowledge, takes note of the evil of men and then brings
inevitable and unexpected judgment upon them (34:25, 26).
Their punishment comes because they refused to follow
God (34:27). One way of refusal is reflected in their cruelty
to the poor (34:28). However, if God remains silent and
does not respond, who has any right to call Him to account
or condemn Him (34:29)? God responds on the basis of the
principle of justice. So, wicked rulers will not succeed because it is not God's purpose for the people to be "ensnared"
or led to ruin by their leaders (34:30).

Obviously with Job in mind, Elihu pointed out the way
the guilty claim their innocence and promise to sin no more
if only someone would point out their sin to them (34:31,
32). But Elihu would have none of this. He called upon
Job to suggest a more equitable method than the one God

uses and thereby to choose his own punishment. As for Elihu, he was content with the one then in use (34:33). Job having made no response, Elihu followed with what he believed the reaction of the wise men would be to Job's arguments (34:34). They would say that he spoke "without knowledge . . . without wisdom" (34:35).

Then, to conclude his second speech, Elihu expressed the hope that Job be "tried unto the end," that is, that he should be tried or afflicted until he had ceased giving answers such as those usually given by guilty men (34:36). By doing so, Job had added defiance ("rebellion") and contempt, shown by "clapping of the hands," to his other sins (34:37). Thus, if anything, Elihu was more severe in his reproach than Eliphaz, Bildad, and Zophar because, in addition to calling upon Job to confess past sins, he charged him with adding to them by refusing to respond, as one should, to the chastening of the Almighty.

3. *Elihu's Claim That Righteousness Makes a Difference* (35:1-16). In his third speech, Elihu attempted to refute Job's argument that righteousness avails nothing and he did so in an unusual way. He stated that heaven is unaffected by man's righteousness or unrighteousness. It is rather man who is affected.

The speech opened with a statement which indicated the part of Job's argument to be dealt with at that point. Job had claimed to have done no wrong, that he was righteous before God, but that it had made no difference (35:2, 3). He would have been just as well off had he sinned, according to this argument. But Elihu challenged Job at this point. And while responding to Job's claim, he would at the same time correct his three friends (35:4).

Taking up the argument which Eliphaz used in 22:12, Elihu told Job to look heavenward and see if he were able to detect any effect of his sin upon the abode of God (35:5, 6). In doing so, he implied that it had not made the slightest difference. Even if man had performed only righteous acts, these would not in the end benefit God (35:7). They

would only benefit man. Only man is the loser from sin
or the one to gain from righteousness (35:8). By this, Elihu
was not suggesting that there was no difference between
good and evil. He was simply arguing that, in the end,
righteousness benefits man just as surely as unrighteousness
harms him.

Following these assertions, Elihu took up the problem of
God's righteousness and the cry of the oppressed (35:9).
"Why, if God rules in righteousness, are men oppressed?"
This question he answered by expressing his belief that it
is because they only call for deliverance from their oppression rather than turning to God and calling upon His mercy
which if they did, He would give them reason to sing His
praise (35:10).

In verse 11, he reminds Job that the birds and beasts can
teach us the ways of God in the world, but that men are
made to be wiser than they, and they should therefore be
wiser. Men should be able to see that suffering is to encour-
age them to call upon God in sincere repentance, not just
to be delivered from the pangs of circumstance (35:12).
It should be obvious to all, especially to Job, that God will
not hear that kind of cry (35:13). On the other hand, if
God will not hear those who do not cry in penitence, He
will surely refuse to listen to those who charge Him with
inconsistency in the way that Job had (35:14).

In verses 15 and 16, Elihu concludes this third speech
with a condemnation of Job's charge that the wicked go
unpunished (see 21:14ff). Evidently, Elihu believed this
heresy was partly the cause of Job's suffering. After all, he
had suggested to those looking on that Job had made one
empty charge after another — charges which reflected upon
his presumed wisdom (35:16). For these, as well as other
sins, Job was now suffering. On this note Elihu's third speech
ended but without an interruption from Job. So, Elihu turned
to his final address.

4. *Elihu's Argument That God's Ways Are Not Past Finding Out* (36:1 — 37:24). Job had implied that God's ways

were beyond human comprehension and, therefore, unjust (see chapter 23). With this in mind, Elihu asked Job to give him a little longer, because he had some more words remaining to be spoken on God's behalf (36:2). He would establish the righteousness of God and he would call upon knowledge "from afar" (36:3). Then, claiming perfect knowledge, he declared that God does not despise any, but takes to heart the case of every man (36:4, 5). He gives to the wicked his just reward and "to the afflicted their right" (36:7). God never takes His eyes off the righteous. Therefore, in addition to being saved from the wicked, the righteous are elevated to the highest positions (36:7). But, if they fall into adversity, it will be for the purpose of showing them their wickedness (36:8, 9) and to teach them as well as to command them to return from their evil ways (36:10). If they respond to His instructions and commands, all will be well with them (36:11, 12). If they refuse, they will suffer and die in the days of their youth just as the wicked always do (36:12-14). On the other hand, if they turn to God when they are afflicted, they will be delivered from their desperate straits and abundantly cared for (36:15, 16).

Then, to apply the case to Job, Elihu told him not to be angry with God when judgments, usually sent upon the wicked, came upon him nor when he realized that the ransom required repentance (36:17, 18). After all, it was in Job's best interest because repentance was the only thing that would avail (36:19). It would do no good to hope for a great national disaster because, if one should come, he could not hope to gain anything from it (36:20). But affliction was something else. Job should have been glad to be afflicted because it gave him his greatest opportunity for deliverance (37:12). After all, God uses His great power to afflict because of the lesson affliction teaches (36:22). God is sovereign, therefore He should not be criticized for what He has done but should be carefully heeded in what He has taught (36:23). It is far wiser to heed God than to criticize Him because, by doing so, God is magnified again as He was when the psalmist and others sang of His greatness

(36:24). They sang of His greatness in spite of His remoteness and their inability to understand Him fully (36:25). By implication, Elihu suggested that Job follow their example.

With the conclusion of his words in which he challenged Job to praise God, Elihu turned to a discussion of God's greatness as revealed in the world of nature. He began this section by stating that God's greatness and eternality transcend man's knowledge (36:26). His greatness is revealed in the wonders of the sky, in the rain, in the thunderstorm and in its effect upon the world of man and nature (36:27 — 37:5). From the activities of the heavens, food in abundance is provided (36:31), the beasts of the field are terrified (36:33) and man is made to tremble (37:1). Elihu called upon Job to listen (37:2-4) in spite of the fact that God's greatness was beyond human comprehension (37:5). But the activity of the heavens was not all. There is the demonstration of God's power in the snow and frost (37:6). When they come, men cease their laboring in the field and, by that, come to know and acknowledge His great power (37:7). The animals go into hibernation (37:8). When the skies express themselves in the storm from the south and in the cold from the north, they but symbolize the breath of God (37:9). They produce ice and frost (37:10). The clouds respond to God's direction and they do so for the purposes of correcting or blessing (37:11-13).

After his lecture on God's greatness as revealed in the world of nature, Elihu called upon Job to be "still and consider the wondrous works of God" (37:14). Then, he asked him how much of it he understood (37:15). He wondered if Job understood "the balancings" or supension of the clouds in the sky (37:16) or if he had observed that man's role is passive in what happens. All he can do is wrap up against the elements (37:17). He cannot spread a sky across the horizon (37:18) and, because of that, the works of God are considered more marvelous. In light of these things, Elihu wished Job to tell him how to address this great God (37:19). He could not imagine himself being presumptuous enough to debate with such a great being because it could mean disaster (37:20).

After these words, Elihu turned back to the marvels of nature, and made an additional reference to the heavens into which they had been looking (37:21). He suggested that if man cannot look upon the brilliance of the sky, after the wind has driven the clouds away, he could never look upon the brightness of God (37:21). That is to say, it would be too presumptuous for Elihu to argue with God. He is too exalted for lowly man. The light of His presence is too brilliant for the failing eyes of lowly man (37:22). Afterwards, Elihu summed up what he had been saying in a few words: "Since God is sovereign and righteous in the universe, it behooves man to fear him rather than to judge him or challenge him because God does not look with favor upon those who are wise in their own eyes" (37:23, 24). By this Elihu was suggesting a great deal; God would consider those of humble heart. By doing this, Elihu was encouraging Job to refrain from any other debate with God. He was being challenged to remember that, after all, he was but a man and that he could never understand the works of God, let alone perform any of them. This much, at least, Job could learn about the ways of God.

FOR FURTHER STUDY

1. Read the article entitled "Elihu" in *IDB*, Volume II, p. 88.

2. How do you explain the paradox seen in Elihu's deference to age and his attitude toward himself? What is your evaluation of Elihu? What problems are you confronted with by him?

3. Read the article entitled "Dream" in *IDB*, Volume I, p. 868 and the one entitled "Dreams" in *DB*, pp. 221, 222.

4. What do you see as Elihu's major contribution to the argument? Discuss.

5. Do you think Elihu was more severe than Job's friends? If so, why? If not, why not?

6. With what did Elihu charge Job's friends? Was he justified in doing so? If not, why not?

CHAPTER 8

The Divine Encounters and Job's Responses

(Job 38:1 — 42:6)

1. Yahweh's Challenges to Job's Presumptuousness (38:1 — 40:2)
2. Job's First Reaction to Yahweh's Questionings (40:3-5)
3. Yahweh's Second Response to Job's Challenge (40:6 — 41:34)
4. Job's Final Words (42:1-6)

This division of the book contains the challenge of Yahweh to Job's presumptuousness. Job had expressed this attitude by contending for his own innocence and challenging Yahweh's righteousness. His friends had sought to help him by arguing that his sufferings were the result of sin. This was the only explanation they could provide. Job rejected their arguments and insisted that he was innocent. He held that if he was being punished for sins he had not committed, then Yahweh's dealings with him were not just. Of course, neither Job nor his friends knew the real cause of his afflictions. They were all ignorant of that, and consequently, they were cut off from the real explanation.

Yahweh had remained silent up to this point. Not a word about His purpose in trying Job had been revealed on earth. In light of this, there are those who believe, and

91

perhaps rightly, that this section serves the purpose of revealing that Job had not been cut off from Yahweh in spite
of His silence. After all, He would now be speaking to him.
Though not answering Job's questions, Yahweh suggested
that He could be trusted and that Job, rather than calling
the Creator to account, should submit to what had happened,
and not continue to resist. Job needed to learn, if he did not
already know, that the Creator is superior to man. Man
in his ignorance should, therefore, remain silent in His presence. Rather than calling Yahweh to justify or even explain
His actions, man should trust Him whether he can understand His actions or not.

1. *Yahweh's Challenges to Job's Presumptuousness* (38:1
— 40:2). Yahweh opened His first speech by challenging
Job's presumptuous spirit and calling him to account. He
answered "out of the whirlwind," in a vision, because man
could not survive a face-to-face confrontation with Him
(38:1) even if innocent. Yahweh asked Job a question. In
it He suggested that He had a purpose in Job's afflictions,
but that Job had misinterpreted, and even obscured it, by
his much speaking, even though he did not know whereof he
spoke (38:2). Therefore, Job was called upon to prepare for
the confrontation which he (Job) had called for in 9:35,
13:22 and elsewhere (38:3).

The encounter actually begins in verse 4. It begins with
a number of questions concerning Job's presumed knowledge. Yahweh asked Job where he was when "the foundations
of the earth" were laid (38:4a). After all, to have challenged
Yahweh, he must have considered himself to be eternal and
omniscient. If he knew all these things, then he ought to
"declare" them (38:4). He ought to be able to answer any
question raised about creation.

Following His first question, Yahweh asked Job about the
boundaries and measures of the earth (38:5) and about the
foundation upon which it rests (38:6, 7). Then, turning from
the earth proper, Yahweh asked about the creation and
bounds of the seas (38:8-11). With each question Job was

made more aware of his human limitations, but Yahweh's inquiries were relentless.

In 38:12-15, Yahweh questions Job about the appearance of day and his role in it. He first asked whether the morning had responded to his command (38:12) or whether he was responsible for the day which had put the wicked to flight (38:13). Following the question about morning, He elaborated upon it. He stated that just as a seal changes the design of the clay, so day changes the formlessness of the night into a multi-colored garment (38:14). Afterward, having returned to His reference to the wicked, He stated that since they look upon darkness as their light, the coming of the day withholds it (their light), and so checks their high-handed activity (38:15).

Next Yahweh inquired about Job's experience with the abode of the deep and his knowledge of Sheol (38:16-17). He insisted that he share his knowledge if he knew about these things (38:18). Job, however, remained in absolute silence. Yet Yahweh pressed on with His examination.

Yahweh's inquiry into Job's knowledge of light and darkness also included information about the dwellings of both (38:19, 20). Surely, Job must know something about that. After all, from the words he had spoken in his arguments, Job must have been living at the time they were set in their places (38:21). It would have been old knowledge to him. He surely had been there at their creation or at least he had entered into the "treasuries" (store-houses of the heavens) where the snow and hail were stored (38:22, 23). Then, having turned back to the light and adding the wind, Yahweh asked him whether he knew how the light and the winds spread across the earth with such great speed (38:24). Again, there is no response from Job.

The next series of questions dealt with the rain and ice. Yahweh asked Job whether he knew who "cleft a channel" in the heavens, to make way for the rains and the lightning, when the earth was drenched (38:25-27). Continuing in this vein, Yahweh, by asking about the father of the rain and the womb of the ice and frost, was inquiring about man's role in the creation of these things (38:28, 29). By this, He was minimizing man's place and reflecting upon Job's presumptuousness. Afterward, He made a statement about the marvels of ice (38:30).

Beginning with verse 31, Yahweh asked Job about his ability to effect what is seen in the appearances of the celestial bodies. Job was asked whether he could bind the Pleiades in a permanent setting as a jeweler placed stones in a necklace or whether he could make possible the free movement of Orion by loosing its belt (38:31). In addition, he was asked whether he could lead forth the signs of the Zodiac as an animal trainer did his animals (38:32), or whether he understood the laws of the heavens well enough to give them directions which would result in the proper effect upon the earth (38:33). Again, as before, the nature of each of the questions suggested that Job did not know enough nor have sufficient power to cause these things.

Yahweh could raise His voice and the heavens would give forth their waters (38:34). Could Job? In verses 35 and 36, Yahweh asked him whether he caused lightning to appear or whether he gave wisdom to the dark clouds. In effect, Yahweh asked him whether he was the one who made possible the wisdom related to the clouds – a wisdom based upon the signs which men saw in the clouds and through which they made judgments and decisions that are here associated with wisdom. Then, as a conclusion to His questions about the clouds, Yahweh inquired whether Job could number the clouds and determine that the proper amount of rain, which in this case was seen contained in bottles, was available to settle the dust of the earth and to soften the hardened clods (38:37-38). As elsewhere, the questions suggest that such abilities are not with man. Since they are not, they could not be possessed by Job. So Job was not as wise as he had presumed when he called the Creator to account.

Beginning with 38:39, which should probably be the beginning of chapter 40, we have the second part of Yahweh's initial speech. It, too, consisted of a series of questions.

Here, the questions related to animal and bird life. They served the same purpose as those in the first part of the speech, which was to reveal to Job the limited capabilities of man and the awesome ability of Yahweh. The first question was about the source of the power which had been given the lion (38:39, 40). The second was whether Job could provide for the raven, the lowliest of birds, when it cried out for food (38:41). The answer suggested to both questions was that no man could do these things. They were the work of Yahweh.

With 39:1 or with verse 4, depending upon where the chapter begins, Job was quizzed about the goat and hind. He was asked whether he knew the exact date they would give birth to their young (39:1-3) or whether he could explain their remarkable ability to provide for their young in such a way as to enable them to mature and look after themselves so soon (39:4).

In verses 5-8, Yahweh asked who sent the donkey into the wilderness and give him his freedom from the throngs of the city or the shouts of a taskmaster. Job remained silent.

Yahweh's next inquiry was about the wild-ox. It, too, was described as strong and free. It was as impossible to harness as the wild donkey. It could never be made content with serving a master (39:9). Therefore, it would be impossible to use it as a plow animal or to depend upon it for bringing in a harvest (39:10-12). As before, the question implied that men had not had anything to do with its creation or its strength.

Verses 13-18, which deal with the ostrich, are missing from the Septuagint and even though in the Masoretic text, they are not in interrogative form. They have, therefore, been rejected by many scholars. Yet there are those who see little to object to, including references to Yahweh in the third person, because they believe it continues to reflect the spirit of the author of Job. If it is by the author and in the proper place, then it adds to the impact of the speech because the point here is the difference between the ostrich and the other birds mentioned. The question of verse 13 suggests this. The wings of the ostrich wave proudly but they cannot lift their bodies into the sky like the wings of the stork do theirs (note marginal reference to verse 13). The ostrich lays her eggs and leaves them for the warmth of the earth to incubate (39:14). She ignores the danger that her nest might be crushed by the animals as they roam about foraging for food (39:15). Her unconcern makes it difficult for her young (39:16), but if her labor to produce young fails, she does not seem to be concerned (39:16). She is a stupid bird. Yahweh has deprived her of wisdom and understanding (39:17), and yet, when she runs ("rouseth up herself") she mocks both horse and rider (39:18). In this case, the point is that, even though the ostrich was denied wisdom, it was given great speed. It had an attribute (speed) which others lacked. That attribute, too, was given by Yahweh. It was not the result of anything man had done.

The mention of the horse in verse 18 is followed by a section characterizing it. Job was asked whether he had given the horse his strength, clothed its neck with a mane, or enabled it to leap as a locust (39:19, 20a). He gave no response. After these questions, there followed a series of descriptive statements about the horse (39:20-21). The horse mocks fear and never flinches before the sword (39:22). As he rushes headlong into battle, the quivers attached to the saddle rattle and the spear and javelin flash as though they were in midair (39:23). His speed is so great that he presents a picture of swallowing the ground as he races along (39:24a). When he hears the trumpet, he can hardly believe that the time to dash forth has come (39:24b). Yet with a satisfying, "Aha!", he dashes off in anticipation of the battle, thrilled to hear the command of his rider (39:25).

Next, Yahweh asked Job whether the hawk migrates to the south when the seasons change as the result of his (Job's) wisdom or whether the eagle builds its nest on the highest crag because Job had commanded it (39:26, 27). Then, by discussing the wisdom of the eagle as shown in her choice of dwellings, Yahweh magnified its quality (39:37, 38). Finally, as a kind of after-thought, a reference was made to the instinct of the eagle as seen in the fact that even their young know how to kill for food (39:30).

In 40:2 Yahweh, as a kind of summary question, asks Job whether he still felt that he (Job) had a basis for contending with Him. Since Job had been unable to answer any of Yahweh's questions positively, it appeared that his effrontery in contending with Yahweh had by now been put into proper focus. If Job expected to be able to challenge Yahweh, he must be able to claim powers equal to His. This Job could not do. He had not even been able to influence the world of nature. How could he expect to debate with nature's Creator?

2. *Job's First Reaction to Yahweh's Questionings* (40:3-5) Having been faced with question after question where he was asked whether in the light of his inability to do any of the things questioned about, he still wanted to correct Yahweh, Job responded with a strong negative answer. He admitted forthwith that he was unable to continue with his challenge. He was "of small account," that is, he had by his actions manifested an attitude which was contemptible (40:4a). To acknowledge this, he placed his hand upon his mouth as a gesture of silence (40:4b). He had already said too much. He had spoken "once," he had spoken "twice," but now he would say no more (40:5). At last, Job was beginning to see the error in what he had done when he challenged Yahweh. This new attitude had resulted from the continuous procession of questions which Yahweh had raised with Job. When he saw the power of Yahweh as revealed in the world of nature, Job saw himself as he really was — a mere man. After that, he had nothing to say. He believed himself to be without the right to speak further.

Job's presumptuousness, however, was not the only thing to receive Yahweh's attention. Job had also challenged His righteousness. Yahweh's reaction to this challenge now followed.

3. *Yahweh's Second Response to Job's Challenge* (40:6 —
41:34). The second response of Yahweh, as the first, was
"out of the whirlwind" (40:6). Whereas the first speech
challenged Job's presumptuous knowledge, the second challenged his charge that Yahweh was unrighteous in His rule
of the world. Yahweh began this speech by calling Job to
prepare for the battle in which some answers would be de-
manded of him (40:7). The very first question raised the
issue of Yahweh's righteousness. Had Job only sought his
own defense, that would have been permitted. But he had
not stopped there. He had gone beyond that and had challenged the justice of Yahweh (40:8b). So Yahweh raised
the question whether, if he had all the other qualifications,
he had the strength ("arm like God") and the ability to
terrify the wicked as He did and, thereby, to take His place
(40:9).

Yahweh continues to challenge Job in verses 10-14. He
called for him to pour out his anger upon the proud and the
wicked in such a way that they would be humbled and
brought to the dust of their graves (40:11-13). When Job
had demonstrated the ability and power to accomplish these
things, then Yahweh would confess, not that Job was worthy
of His place as might be expected, but only that he would be
able to deliver himself (40:14).

The remainder of the second speech consists of a description of the power of Yahweh as depicted in His creation of
the hippopotamus and leviathan (the crocodile). Many
scholars claiming these discussions to be irrelevant to the
main emphasis of this section believe them to be a later in-
sertion. Yet this has been challenged by those who believe
they are in keeping with the context.

The first of the two to be considered was "behemoth" or,
as the marginal note suggests, the "hippopotamus." Job's
attention was now turned to the hippopotamus which, along
with himself, had been made by Yahweh (40:15). Its
strength is reflected in the muscles of its loins and stomach
(40:16). The rigidity of its tail is to be compared with that
of a cedar tree, the sinews of its thighs are described as hav-

ing been carefully and wonderfully knit together (40:17) and the bones which make up his skeleton are described as being as strong as "tubes of brass" and "bars of iron" (40:18).

This remarkable creature is designated "the chief," literally, "the beginning of God's creation." By this Yahweh meant that the hippopotamus is the most powerful of the creation (40:19). A part of its power lies in its great horn ("sword") (40:19b). As far as its needs are concerned, it requires the vegetation of entire mountain ranges (40:20). Upon being satisfied, it seeks out the shade and cool of any remaining plants and lies down (40:21, 22). This great beast is fearless. The floods of the rainy season present him with no terror (40:23). He is not afraid of being captured. He could not, in fact, be taken like any other ordinary animal. He is a wary creature who spurns the efforts of would-be captors (40:24).

Certainly the point of the preceding section was to challenge Job further at the point of his own power. The question implied was whether he had the power to create such a monster. The answer would have to be a negative one. But wait, Yahweh had not finished.

Chapter 41 contains an account of Yahweh's power as seen in "leviathan," the crocodile. The first question had to do with Job's ability to catch one with a fish hook (41:1) and bind its mouth with a rope (41:2). Then, in words of irony, Job was asked whether he believed the crocodile would seek gentle treatment by soft words (41:3) or whether it would make a covenant and become an obedient slave (41:4), to which the obvious answer was, "No!" Continuing in this negative vein, it was also suggested, by a series of questions, that Job would not make it a pet (41:5, 6). Neither would fishermen barter over one that had been caught (41:7) because it could not be speared and handled as the fish after it was caught (41:8). Any and all who hoped to overcome this creature would meet with inevitable disappointment (41:9). No one is fierce enough to survive a match with him.

Verses 10 and 11 turn aside from the main argument. Their purpose is to teach the lesson of leviathan. That lesson is, if

man would not venture to stir up this creature which God
had made, who would presume to call its Creator to account?
After all, no one had any reason to do so. The Creator had
received nothing from the hand of anyone nor did He have
any need to. The whole creation was His! Why would He
need to ask anything of man, whom He had created?

With verse 12, the description of the crocodile resumes.
Yahweh did not intend to remain silent because this remarkable creature provided such a good point in His argument.
Therefore, He continued to probe Job with questions concerning man's inability in the face of the strength of the
crocodile. Yahweh asked Job whether anyone could strip
off his scales (41:13) or force him to open his terrible
mouth (41:14).

The pride of the crocodile is in his scales which are so
joined together that air cannot pass through (41:15-17).
When it sneezes, the spray from his nostrils appears to be
flashes of light (41:18). When it emerges from the water,
its breath is blown from its mouth and it appears as though
it were the jet of a fiery stream (41:19-21). The neck of the
crocodile, elsewhere believed to be the seat of strength,
evokes terror in those who come upon it (41:22). The flakes,
that part under the crocodile's neck and stomach, are not
soft as are those of other animals; in him they are muscular
and firm (41:23). His heart is as hard as the "nether millstone" (41:24). The "nether millstone," because it receives
all of the weight of grinding, needs to be stronger and
harder than the upper millstone. Even the strongest of men
are frightened by the crocodile (42:25). It is more than
a match for the sword, spear, dart or pointed shaft (42:26).
Iron is like straw and brass is as brittle as decayed wood
when he bites down upon it (42:27). Neither the arrow,
the slingstone, the club nor the javelin cause him any fear
(41:28, 29). His most vulnerable parts are as hard as pot-
sherds (41:30a). Wherever he lies there remains an impression of his body as vivid as if it had been made in the
earth by the sharp teeth of a threshing instrument (41:30b).
When he rolls in the deep, the waters foment like those in

a boiling kettle of water or ointment being prepared for use (41:31). His racing through the water leaves a shining path after him and one would think the sea hoary on account of the foam left in his wake (41:32). There is no other creature so fearless (41:33). He looks upon all who would presumably be above or over him and dominates them by the fear which he evokes (41:34). He is indeed a powerful creature. Could Job create a creature like that? Upon this note, Yahweh concluded His speaking and we have but to hear from Job.

4. *Job's Final Words* (42:1-6). Though many would connect these verses with 40:5 and make them a continuation of Job's response to Yahweh's first speech, thereby treating his second speech as secondary, others see in it an advance in Job's feeling toward Yahweh as well as toward himself.

Job's reaction to Yahweh's second speech reflected a deeper awareness of His greatness. He confessed his belief in Yahweh's ability to do whatever He willed and acknowledged that He could not be denied the realization of anything which He purposes (42:2). Job went beyond this, however, and echoed the words of Yahweh in 38:2. In doing so, he set the context for additional words of confession. These followed as Job acknowledged that he had obscured knowledge by uttering those things which he did not understand or which were too wonderful for him (38:3). In doing so, he was evidently referring to the mistaken judgments he had spoken about Yahweh's purposes in the incidents which had taken place in his life as well as the rash statements he had made.

In verse 4, Job repeated the words of Yahweh found in 38:3 and 40:7 and then answered in verse 5. In other words, having repeated Yahweh's challenge to Job to speak, he responded in a very unusual way. He as much as said, "Lord, You said, 'Hear . . . and declare unto me,' but after seeing You as You really are, rather than as I have been taught that You are, I repudiate what I have said and repent in sackcloth and ashes" (42:5, 6).

By his confession Job acknowledged that his understanding, the understanding expressed in his arguments, was based
upon what he had been taught. He now saw Yahweh as
being too great to be pressed into the narrow limits of the
human mind. Therefore, he repudiated all that he had said
about and to Yahweh. He repented "in dust and ashes." For
his repentance to take this form, meant that he was humbling
himself before Yahweh as one bowed down with a grief
that could not be assuaged. In other words, his repentance
was genuine and his sorrow continuous. He would never
again be guilty of past follies. In the future he would acknowledge Yahweh on the basis of the experience gained
by having seen Him and he would refrain from calling Him
to account. He saw Him as being too great for man's presumptuous spirit. Man's place before Him was one of
submission and silence! Otherwise, he would be called to
account and brought to repentance as Job had been in the
section just discussed. Yet, with all of the faults acknowledged by Job, it must be remembered that he had not
cursed Yahweh. He had complained to Him, even debated
with Him, but he had not fulfilled Satan's prediction that
he would curse Yahweh. The idea had never entered his
mind. He could never be brought to that.

In the future, Job would never again challenge Yahweh.
He would suffer in silence, if suffer he must, because God
was too great to have to justify His dealings with the lives
of His creatures.

Not only was Yahweh too great to be challenged, His ways
which are past finding out, must be accepted as just. In
Job's case, Yahweh had a reason, known only to Himself and
the angels, for Job's suffering. It was a divine reason and
not a human reason which had brought Job's trouble upon
him. For that reason Job's reaction was so reprehensible.
Therefore, when men suffer, and know not why, there always remains that same possibility for them. That being so,
man must trust God and submit to the circumstances of life
in faith and love.

For Further Study

1. Read the article entitled "God, O.T. View of" in *IDB*, Volume II, pp. 417-430 and the one entitled "God" in *DB*, pp. 333-337.

2. Which attribute(s) of Job do you think the speeches of Yahweh reflect upon?

3. Which of Job's arguments did this confrontation with Yahweh disprove?

4. Did Job react to Yahweh's speeches as you had anticipated? Would you have been as submissive as he was? Have you ever been? What were the circumstances of your experience?

5. What lesson do you see being taught by the speeches of Yahweh?

6. What form of reasoning did Yahweh use to convince Job? Do you use it in your dealing with men? Has it been effective?

CHAPTER 9
The Epilogue
(Job 42:7-17)

1. Job's Vindication and His Friends' Censure (42:7-9)
2. The Restoration of Job (42:10-17)

After Job's response in 42:1-7, there follows the epilogue which has been questioned by many Old Testament scholars. Some argue that this section mars the book by verifying the argument of the friends, while others contend that this is not the case at all. For them, the epilogue substantiates the contention that there is such a thing as disinterested righteousness. Therefore, the epilogue is considered essential. In either eventuality, the story would be incomplete, even pointless, without the conclusion found in 42:7-17. The very nature of the problem of Job requires that the man, who has not fulfilled Satan's prophecy, be released from his afflictions and that he be rewarded for his faithfulness. The epilogue furnishes that requirement.

1. *Job's Vindication and His Friends' Censure* (42:7-9). Following Job's statement of confession and repentance, Yahweh turned His attention to Job's three friends. He spoke to Eliphaz, but included the other two, Bildad and Zophar, in his statement of censure (42:7a). They were censured

for having spoken wrongly for God (42:7b). Though many of the things spoken by Job's friends were true, there was an overriding falseness in what they had said. Their theories about God's providence and the meaning of suffering were not true in themselves. To be sure, suffering may result from sin, but to say that all suffering is caused by sin, as Job's friends had charged, was not borne out by the facts. By insisting that it was, they were misrepresenting God all the while they were presuming to defend Him. Though Job did not know why he was subjected to pain and suffering, he denied that it was because of the sins with which they had charged him. In doing so, and even while charging Yahweh with injustice, he was nearer the truth than his friends had been. They had spoken wrongly *for* God while Job had only spoken wrongly *of* God. But, had Job known that he was the victim of a trial permitted by Yahweh, for the purpose of proving that there was a disinterested goodness, then his whole attitude would have been quite different. On the other hand, had Job known the whole truth, then the purpose of the book would have been lost. As it was, Job had vindicated Yahweh's claim to Satan. Through his confession and repentance, he was himself vindicated.

As for Job's friends, they were commanded to make a large offering to atone for their wrongs and to await the prayers of Job (42:8). Their so doing would result in Yahweh's not dealing with them on the basis of their folly, but in accordance with His mercy. His mercy would be based, at least in part, upon the intercession of Job. This is made clear in the latter part of verse 9 where it states that Yahweh accepted Job, that is, he responded to Job's intercession. Thus, both Job and his friends find their standing with God altered and in both cases it was because of His mercy.

2. *The Restoration of Job* (42:10-17). With Job's vindication and the disappearance of the friends, the book returns to Job. First, Yahweh restored his fortune and doubled it (42:10). After that, Job's friends and family gathered about him to express their sympathy and concern (42:11a). They

gave him money and rings of gold as tokens of their joy over his return to health and good fortune (42:11b). Job's second fortune included 14,000 sheep, 6,000 camels, 1,000 oxen and 1,000 she-asses (42:12) and, best of all, seven more sons and three more daughters (42:13).

Though Job's sons are not named, his daughters are. The names of the daughters were: Jemimah, which probably means "dove"; Keziah, which means "sweet" or "fragrant"; and Keren-happuch, which seems to mean "horn of eye paint" (42:14). These three were, as their names seem to suggest, very beautiful. They were, in fact, the most beautiful in the land (42:15a).

Justifiably proud of his family, and hoping to keep them happily united, even after his death, Job gave each of them, sons and daughters alike, an inheritance (42:15b). This was an exception to common practice. Usually, daughters were excluded from an inheritance unless they were from a family without sons (see Numbers 27:1ff.). Job's action indicated his hope, yea, even his intention, that the happy relations which his children had known in their youth would continue in their adulthood.

The concluding two verses of the book tell of Job's long and happy life. He lived one hundred and forty years after his restoration, long enough to see his seed to the fourth generation (42:16). He died having lived a long, full and satisfying life (42:17). On this note of triumph, the book of Job closes.

Recounted herein is the story of one of the world's most remarkable men. It is the story of his struggle to understand life, which he finally did when he submitted completely and without question to his Lord. May his number increase!

FOR FURTHER STUDY

1. Which, according to the book of Job, is more reprehensible, speaking wrongly of God or for God? Why do you think one a greater evil than the other?

2. Having read the book of Job, how many different ap-

proaches to the problem of suffering does it suggest? List
all you can recall.

3. How would you evaluate the various approaches to
suffering found in Job? Are certain ones more valid than
others? If so, why? If not, why not?

4. Is there a possible relationship between the length
and happiness of life and a man's attitude toward life and
God? Was such a relationship suggested by Job's long and
full life? Discuss.